LORD BYRON IN VENICE

Borgo Press Books Edited & Translated by FRANK J. MORLOCK

LORD BYRON IN VENICE

A Play in Three Acts

by

Jacques Ancelot

Translated and Adapted by Frank J. Morlock

The Borgo Press

An Imprint of Wildside Press LLC

MMX

CONTENTS

DEDICATION

To

Dan Woloshen

Who would have made a great Byron

CAST OF CHARACTERS

LORD BYRON

TRELAWNEY, his friend, a corsair

COUNT OROBONI, A Venetian noble.

DE SENNEVILLE, a young Frenchman

AN ENGLISHMAN

WILLIAM, Byron's valet

LADY BYRON

COUNTESS OROBONI, the Count's wife

MARGARITA COGNI (called GUITTA) a woman of the
  people

LADY MILWOOD

AN AUSTRIAN OFFICER

ITALIANS, ENGLISHMEN, AND SERVANTS

ACT I

The stage represents a terrace which connects the Oroboni palace to another building that is almost opposite. To the audience left, on the front of this building can be read "Grande Albergo del Leone de San Marco", The Palazzo Oroboni situated facing it, to the audience's right, has two doors opening on the terrace, and the one closest to the audience is open. Near this door, on the terrace, is a divan and other seats. At the rear of the stage, there reigns a balustrade split in the middle by a stairway whose steps lead to the water of the canal. In the distance, behind this balustrade, the Tower: one side represents a line of palaces and buildings lost in the distance, and on the other, the sea and vessels.

Lady Milwood is at the back leaning on the balustrade.

COUNTESS OROBONI: (seated on the couch by the door of her palace, to herself) What a delightful night! These great palaces which are only the devastated remains of Venetian grandeur bring you the spreading centuries and deliver the soul to a profound reverie! I'm not surprised that Byron came here to seek new emotions and to forget the pains of life! All small cares are effaced by this grand spectacle. As for myself, I no longer recall anything except the sporadic amusements which intoxicated me in Paris. Here I no longer dare to think of such frivolous pleasures, of beauty so fragile, of coquetting so flighty! And yet, I'm wrong. Fear this burning, these profound emotions! Let's keep my heart calm in this country of fiery passions! Mad distractions come to the aid of my wisdom, and save my heart from the danger of reflecting; because love is terrible here. And Byron is in Venice.

LADY MILWOOD: (in the distance) Once again that lovely barcarole which we so often hear.

COUNTESS: Doubtless it's the signal of love. In this beautiful land life has but one object: happiness, and it's almost always attained.

LADY MILWOOD: Then you don't regret France, my dear Countess?

COUNTESS: Can one have regrets under a heaven so pure and so sweet? And you, milady, are you still thinking of England?

LADY MILWOOD: I don't regret it but I always love it

COUNTESS: That voice is familiar to me.

LADY MILWOOD: Let's listen!

GUITTA: (singing in the wings)

Let's sing the barcarolle.
Spice improves work
For pleasure steals away
More promptly than a gondola
Sliding through the water.
Listen in the plain
Joyous songs!
The hour of night brings
Our honey.
Let's all pray to the Madonna.
It's she who gives
Flowers whose scent embalms our feet!
Let our hand pick them
Let love embloom them!
The Italian fields won't be crushed.
Let's sing the barcarolle.

COUNTESS: The song's stopping.

LADY MILWOOD: The gondola's stopping at the foot of this stairway, a woman's climbing up.

COUNTESS: Ah! I recognize her. It's the Fornarina Margarita Coqui.

LADY MILWOOD: Of whom I've heard you speak so often.

(Enter Guitta, basket in hand)

GUITTA: Herself, and who's devoted to you entirely, Madame Countess, because she hasn't forgotten the services you rendered her and if she is able—

COUNTESS: Nothing, Guitta, nothing at all! A little money, what's that. Haven't you paid me with attachment? I'm the one who owes you something. But here it's a month since you've come to the palace Oroboni; that's bad.

GUITTA: (sighing) You say the truth.

COUNTESS: Then go in, Guitta, and come back.

(Guitta goes into the palazzo)

LADY MILWOOD: I'm not surprised if I haven't yet seen her because it is only a month since I arrived in Venice!

COUNTESS: Yes, and it is at this period, that at your recommendation, I have plucked up Lord Byron your illustrious patriot.

LADY MILWOOD: (aside) If she knew that, it is for him alone that I've come.

COUNTESS: I agreed to cede to him this whole section of the vast Palazzo Oroboni, so bad to dwell in alone, but very pleasant since you have chosen for your dwelling this hotel Lion of Saint Mark where distinguished foreigners stay.

LADY MILWOOD: Thanks to this terrace, we are almost lodged together.

COUNTESS: That's so.

LADY MILWOOD: Our curiosity is vividly excited by a foreigner debarking here two days ago, everything is mysterious about that woman, she's constantly shut in, she never sees anybody.

COUNTESS: Her secrets must be respected. Don't we have our own?

LADY MILWOOD: That's just.

COUNTESS: This hotel, that inn, to be more precise, were formerly part of the dwelling of my husband, Count Oroboni's ancestors. But truly, it would seem that men of our century are much too small for the vast dwellings of their ancestors. What has caused changes in their ideas and in their fortunes so that descendants of these illustrious and powerful Venetians have reached the point of delivering to all comers, their sumptuous dwellings, where they let them bask every day under their eyes?

GUITTA: (returning and hearing the last phrase) Ah! You are speaking of our poor Italy. Freedom will return to it all that slavery lost.

LADY MILWOOD: Margarita is right to hope.

COUNTESS: Perhaps! But I shall not say less. It's not the time of palaces. In France they are seen to be demolished; in Venice they are seen to crumble.

LADY MILWOOD: In France as in Venice I admire in you the likable and observant wit that charms and amuses me. How lucky I am once again to find here an acquaintance who gave so much delight in Paris three years ago.

COUNTESS: At that time you were already a widow, and I was not yet married.

LADY MILWOOD: I was seeking to distract myself from the boredom of widowhood.

COUNTESS (smiling) How many balls, parties, shows we needed against that pain. You recollect? But the means succeeded so well for us, that as for me, I employ it every day.

LADY MILWOOD: But you are not a widow.

COUNTESS: Perhaps that's why.

LADY MILWOOD: What do I hear? Aren't you happy with Count Oroboni?

COUNTESS: Oh, my God, yes! Although I am French, my mother, following the arrangements of fortune, had promised me to the Count who is Italian: I didn't know him. He came, took me without knowing me, and we had no other acquaintance except to find ourselves married one fine day! Two years ago he led me to Venice; he gives me no real subject of complaint but he hardly seems concerned with his marriage.

LADY MILWOOD: Truly?

COUNTESS: In Oroboni's soul there's a passion absorbs everything, which passes before his love affairs, before his interests, before his pleasures. He loves Italy, his enslaved country, and this feeling in him has all the strength of an unfortunate and thwarted passion. He lives for it, vows, plans, hopes—his Italian pride disdains, to associate in it the woman that he has for company, and as for me, I do not solicit the confidence he refuses me. Thus we find ourselves divided by ideas and customs. Almost no one ever sees us together, and sometimes I surprise myself saying "Who is this foreigner really, that I am married to?"

LADY MILWOOD: How happy you are, you French women, to take the gravest matters of life so lightly.

GUITTA: (to the Countess) They say that in your country, they don't know how to love or to hate.

COUNTESS: (smiling) Do you think that's a bad thing?

GUITTA: Yes. It's not living.

COUNTESS: Do you hear her, Milady? Margarita expresses herself so excitedly that she always astonishes me!

It would be really worse if she had a passion.

GIUITTA: (laughing) Well, the worst has arrived.

COUNTESS: (laughing) Truly, Guitta?

GUITTA: And that's why for the last month I haven't had time to come to the Oroboni palace.

LADY MILWOOD: I would be curious to know the object of her choice.

COUNTESS: Come, Guitta, make us your confidants. That ought to be fun.

GUITTA: (excitedly) Poor Guitta is completely devoted to you, Countess, but she is not delivering the secret of her heart to the vanity of great ladies.

LADY MILWOOD: Pardon, Margarita.

GUITTA: Yes, you are rich and titled, but I am Venetian you understand.

COUNTESS: Hey, there, darling. We are all three young women who enjoy talking of love. That's all. No one wanted to offend you, Guitta.

GUITTA: By the Madonna, you would make me your confidant, too?

LADY MILWOOD: Why not, if we had something to confide.

GUITTA: (cleverly) Hell! If you told the whole truth perhaps.

COUNTESS: No question thee have been some sighs, but that doesn't count.

GUITTA: (laughing) Oh! Really! With me everything counts. But if I'm not mistaken this pretty lady with her very sweet manner is not so calm in the depths of her heart as she would like to appear.

LADY MILWOOD: (sighing) Me?

GUITTA: Come on! Come on! I've just heard a sigh which might pass for a confidence. As for Madame Countess, I think she actually has nothing to hide unless it's the plan of turning all our heads, without risking her own.

(going between them) Well, I won't make mysteries. You will have all my secrets.

COUNTESS: Great!

GUITTA: Conceive that each morning for the last month I've seen pass before my hut a man whose face struck me from the very beginning. One day, surprised by the rain, around three weeks ago, he came in to ask me for shelter.

Hardly had he seen me than he stopped, astonished, and as for me, I felt uneasy and seized at the mere sound of his voice! We were looking like that in silence and we are in love immediately, lovers for life!

LADY MILWOOD: And then, no doubt you told him that?

GUITTA: Oh, there was no need to tell him; he's saw it before I did.

COUNTESS: Who then is this shy conqueror?

GUITTA: I don't know exactly, but I think he's a hunter from around here. I've seen him often returning from the woods with game, like his friend who accompanies him. Oh, he's not handsome and fair like your lovers. My friend loves to climb mountains, escarpments, to tame a foaming wild horse, to corse the seas swimming despite the winds and contrary waves.

LADY MILWOOD: I confess, I'd be terrified of such a savage conflict.

GUITTA: I bet my gold cross that the one who pleases you won't be as good as my Nolly.

LADY MILWOOD: The one that I love. Must it be admitted that I love?

GUITTA: Come on! Can it be otherwise?

LADY MILWOOD: The one who is dear to me is given over, as I am, to the dreams of his imagination, finding no charm in glory; never have his delicate hands attempted rough and crude work; it's his burning soul, his brilliant and profound thought which he's pleased to exercise and his genius is animated and developed in calm and solitude.

GUITTA: This lady is foreign?

COUNTESS: English.

GUITTA: Ah, then that's it.

COUNTESS: (smiling) You don't understand. But I, too, Guitta, have ideas that differ greatly from yours. It's necessary to please me, if a contract had not formerly confiscated to Count Oroboni's profit all my rights to love and happiness along with the two hundred thousand francs of my dowry; it would be necessary, I say, not for Guitta, your wild friend, accustomed to violent exercises of a life of noise and motion, nor at all; or your melancholy and impassioned dreamer, Milady—but a friendly and happy dandy, absorbing gaily the follies and quirks of man, loaning himself to the customs of society, all in doing them justice by making them know how to chat maliciously, and I don't say he cannot enjoy a fine horse, or defend his ideas or his affections courageously, but above all, he must have worldly graces.

GUITTA: Ah, leave that! Is it for that one is in love? If he really is amorous, he will know enough about it.

COUNTESS: (smiling) Our ideas are so different that we will never be rivals.

GUITTA: No, for sure! Imagine my lover hurling himself on a rocky escarpment to come kiss me at the moment in which I think he's very far off, or diving into the Brenta to find the kiss I sent him from the other bank.

LADY MILWOOD: And my poet: behold him dreaming up a better world, so as to place our dreams of love there, too pure and too sweet for this one.

COUNTESS: Who wouldn't admire in the midst of a brilliant circle that mills about the better to hear him, the ingenious wit and the thousand pithy sayings of the man who sometimes occupies my thoughts?

GUITTA: As for me, I will not forgive the slightest infidelity.

LADY MILWOOD: Nor I!

COUNTESS: As for me,—I don't know!

GUITTA: Inconstancy and forgetfulness! That would really be worse, if my lover left me for a rival.

COUNTESS: Well?

LADY MILWOOD: As for me, I'd die of sorrow.

GUITTA: Me, I'd kill him.

COUNTESS: And I, I think—that—

GUITTA: That you would love some one else.

COUNTESS: That's possible.

LADY MILWOOD: Ah!

COUNTESS: Well, since we've gone so far, a complete confidence. The name of the one you love, Milady?

GUITTA: Yes, yes! I have nothing to hide. Speak, my ladies! His name?

LADY MILWOOD: (hesitating) His name?

COUNTESS: (hesitating) His name?

A SERVANT: (announcing) Lord Byron.

LADY MILWOOD: Lord Byron.

COUNTESS: (aside) It's him.

GUITTA: (at the moment Byron appears) Nolly, here!

(Enter Trelawney and Byron)

BYRON: (low, smiling, to Trelawney) All three.

(aloud, advancing) Countess Oroboni has deigned to permit me the honor of presenting my friend Trelawney to her.

COUNTESS: You know, Milord, how much I desired it.

GUITTA: (aside, stupefied) Milord?

TRELAWNEY: (to the Countess) Please be so good, Madame, as to accept all my thanks.

COUNTRESS: (to Lady Milwood) Milady, you have heard tell of the adventurous life of your compatriot, and of the incredible courage he displayed in so many excursions? So many years spent at sea.

TRELAWNEY: Hey! What else would I have done?

GUITTA: (aside) Nolly, milord? And he alone doesn't notice it!

BYRON: (with a bitter irony) Conqueror or pirate, right Trelawney? That's the way to live. But to vegetate in the midst of the world, to spend one's energy under the yoke which the majority of dumb-bells impose on all that do not resemble themselves compromises the spirit of one's thought and the movements of one's soul. Now that, for sure, is a struggle less painful and less glorious than that wherein each day one is guiding his ship through a tempest, a battle or a reef. For our compatriot, my lady no longer needs praise England, he is like me! The nation doesn't treat him like a spoiled child.

TRELAWNEY: And we treat it like ungrateful children.

GUITTA: (aside) I don't know what to think. I am having trouble containing myself.

LADY MILWOOD: Oh! You haven't abandoned her forever.

BYRON: Forever, milady! My old castle remains deserted.

GUITTA: (aside) His castle!

BYRON: The brambles are growing in the avenue. And the solitary dog hurls itself at the gate forever locked.

TRELAWNEY: As for me, except for some blows of the fist and some kicks, I received nothing from my respectable family. I have neither land nor castles to regret, not even a dog.

BYRON: So much the better for you! If I return to my domain, mine might come and bite me.

COUNTESS: Ah, why, milord, are you pleased to destroy our illusions? Allow us some hope in our friendship, not just dogs.

BYRON: (in an affectionate tone) You have nothing to

fear, Madame. Indeed, you will find attachment much in accord with your wishes,

GUITTA: (aside) The way he's looking at her!

LADY MILWOOD: Milord, I was expecting you this morning.

COUNTESS: Ah—

BYRON: Affairs without number—

CUITTA: (coming close to him) Who are you, really? These ladies call you "Milord". You talk of castles.

BYRON: (in a low voice) Hush!

TRELAWNEY: (low to Guitta) He will explain it all to you.

LADY MILWOOD: (to Byron) You know this young girl?

TRELAWNEY: (quickly) In our strolls through Venice we've sometimes met.

COUNTESS: What! Could it be?

GUITTA: Ah, Madame.

BYRON: (gesturing to Guitta to shut-up; she stops) The

moment is difficult.

COUNTESS: But would it actually be possible? No, it's madness.

LADY MILWOOD: What have you conjectured?

COUNTESS: I was thinking that these gentlemen who run through the world to seek adventures, pleasures, thrills and success, had, perhaps, found on the shores of the Brenta, at last the man Guitta was talking of just now.

LADY MILWOOD: Is that believable? The portrait she drew doesn't resemble that which I myself sketched of Milord.

GUITTA: (aside) She was talking about him!

TRELAWNEY: (aside) This is going to cause trouble. Let's try to change the subject.

(aloud) What an evening, ladies. What a sight for eyes, accustomed to the sad and leaden atmosphere of London.

GUITTA: Go, our Italian hearts resemble still less the hearts of your frigid English! They don't know how to contain what they are feeling.

TRELAWNEY: It's not always prudent to tell everything.

GUITTA: Nor easy to hide everything.

LADY MILWOOD: No, no.

(in a rage) For all is discovered in the end and one can learn—

BYRON: (in a mocking tone) What then, milady?

COUNTESS: They contend in England that oft times in Paris a woman of fashion sees near her the man who pleased her, the one who now pleases her, and the one who will please her. I deny that such a thing can be met with in our country, and wouldn't be much a surprised if it was not a woman who found herself in that situation.

BYRON: Could such a thing be?

LADY MILWOOD: (sharply) Why not? They indeed say that in France that the English are models of constancy and fidelity.

COUNTESS: (laughing) Now, observe how seven leagues of channel between two countries can falsify all ideas!

GUITTA: Ah, indeed! For the last hour, I looked, I listened, and I barely comprehended. Who are you? Have I been deceived to the point of not even suspecting to whom I gave my heart?

LADY MILWOOD: (aside) Is he the one?

COUNTESS: (aside) Oh, my beautiful dreams!

TRELAWNEY: We are navigating in the midst of a storm!

GUITTA: What storm are you talking about? I ought to have left you exposed a thousand times rather than enter my poor hut! Oh, it was useless for you to try to impose silence on me! I cannot be calm when my happiness is threatened, when I don't know what to think of the one I love, when perhaps I'm being deceived, betrayed. Because it's he, Madame, my Nolly! My love, my happiness, my life, he at last!

(She goes to Byron and grabs his hand)

LADY MILWOOD: (wrathfully) Well, my Lord?

BYRON: Well, my Lady?

TRELAWNEY: Give yourself the trouble of hiding a secret three weeks.

GUITTA: (looking at the ladies, one after the other) I've seen everything! Everything is explained to me now! This dreamy poet, that's him, too! This brilliant and witty man, as you said, that was him again! But who is he who can be loved by such different tastes, the one that poor Guitta took for her equal, whose genius Milady boasted of, and that you call "Milord"?

COUNTESS: It's Lord Byron.

GUITTA: Byron!

BYRON: (laughing) You don't know who he is, Guitta?

GUITTA: I know that I am wretched.

BYRON: Why? Is it because the voice of the one who told you "I love you" has also pronounced speeches to the Parliament of England where he ranks among the peers? Go, cheer up! They simply didn't understand me; and I've renounced that honor. I don't want a throne purchased by boredom. Perhaps, Guitta, they also told you, that a poetic celebrity is attached to my name, and you didn't understand? So much the better! You will learn that I am the prey of the first paper peddler who thinks he has the right to tell me insults at so much per page! You think I'm amused by that? No, my poor Guitta, no! The one in whom I placed my happiness has rejected me with words of hate! Go, fear nothing, you who loved me for myself, without knowing that I was Byron! Come, stay close to me. Your smile consoles me for what they call my fortune and my glory.

LADY MILWOOD: (aside) If I am able to get revenge one day—!

COUNTESS: (aside) Luckily, I kept my heart.

TRELAWNEY: (to Byron) Here comes company! It will be a diversion.

GUITTA: He loves me! Come on! No chagrin, whoever you may be, my happiness comes from you, and my life belongs to you.

(Meanwhile, the Countess and Lady Milwood cross the stage and greet the guests who are arriving. Enter Count Oroboni and Mr. de Senneville)

COUNT: Pardon for interrupting a conversation.

BYRON: The subject of which was not to everyone's taste, but may be vividly appreciated by you, Count.

COUNT: These ladies will actually accept my homage?

(to Trelawney) I am charged to again meet with the intrepid traveler, his courage, perhaps, will not be amiss here! Hello, Guitta!

(to Byron) Now there, Milord is a real Italian girl. Society and fashion are wasted on most great foreign ladies. The Italian face and heart are preserved in their purity under their custom.

(to the Countess) But, my dear friend, you begged your compatriot, Mr. de Senneville to escort you to the ball, and it seems to me you have forgotten.

COUNTESS: I confess, at the moment, I wasn't thinking about it at all.

SENNEVILLE: As for me, I was on time—for the first time!

(looking at his watch) An hour late, but that's nothing much. Why there's so little freedom. And besides, who thinks of time?

COUNTESS: You want to make us think you are contemplating things more important than the ball?

SENNEVILLE: Oh! Who's pleased by the ball? Who can endure these vulgar amusements? For me, for a long time now, returned from pleasures, life seems to me just a very tiresome thing. And love? Love! Who can still believe in that?

(to Byron) Isn't it true, Milord, that poets like us, exiled in this world, never find anything which can satisfy our heart?

BYRON: Speak for yourself, sir.

SENNEVILLE: What do you mean? Haven't you expressed this weariness of life in admirable verse? This boredom with success that man experiences at the height of faculties placed above his peers, or the devouring passions that have blazed on vulgar pleasures? How to comply with foolish social customs at these monotonous balls, at these insipid visits? Can you live an ordinary life like the rest?

COUNT: (smiling) It seems to me that before the arrival of milord in Venice you were very happy in it, and that even yesterday, at dinner, you managed dining life very easily.

COUNTESS: Then why, at the age of pleasures without any chagrin affecting you, are you to proclaim this singular distance?

SENNEVILLE: He who has felt all, experienced all the cheating joys of this world, remains sad and withered.

BYRON: When will you reach your majority, Mr. De Senneville?

SENNEVILLE: In eighteen months, milord! But years are counted by ideas, by sensation, and like Lara, I am really old.

COUNTESS: (smiling) Lara, that's it! Truly, men of genius must take care of those for whom they write because they are responsible for many stupidities.

COUNT: Alas, why lose a precious life in inaction? This futile life, these frivolous pleasures, I am not astonished that they bore you. Employ your life in glorious enterprises.

SENNEVILLE: Ah!

COUNT: Listen to me. Here we have the need of courage

and strength. Trelawney, can I count on you?

TRELAWNEY: If you have danger to offer me, here I am! Because I already feel the boredom of rest.

COUNT: Mr. De Senneville, I will reveal to you pleasures over which you can be at ease.

(to Byron) Milord, when one possesses the greatest literary glory of the century, does there remain one desire?

BYRON: Count, what is it to write in these times in which we live? What is a literary reputation in a century that has seen Napoleon?

COUNT: He resounds, it's true.

BYRON: (sadly) He put a period to all past glory and made impossible all glory to come.

COUNTESS: (to Lady Milwood) Just like I told you, Milady, here my husband comes and politics comes with him.

(they speak in whispers distancing themselves)

COUNT: He really knew how to conquer nations; but perhaps there remains one thing more to do.

TRELAWNEY: What's that?

COUNT: (in a whisper) To free them.

BYRON: Hush! Count!

TRELAWNEY: My arm is at your service.

BYRON: (to the Count) It doesn't suffice that an enterprise be just and holy: it must still be possible.

COUNT: We've been thinking about it for a long while; everything is prepared, the most noble families, the most distinguished writers—

BYRON: That are already victims.

COUNT: Each martyr of liberty makes children new partisans

BYRON: Here courage is only in the higher ranks. You have only officers and no army. You must wait.

COUNT: We have waited too long.

(in a low voice) Tomorrow a new attempt to direct—

BYRON: (taking his hand) To direct? To command?

COUNT: The post I am directed to offer you. Your high renown....

BYRON: (joyfully) Ah, at last. Count, my fortune and my life for your liberty.

COUNT: Tomorrow you will know all our plans.

BYRON: Tomorrow. Tomorrow, perhaps, we will exchange our pen for a sword!

(to De Senneville) Meanwhile, Mr. de Senneville, I advise you to go to the ball and amuse yourself like a simple mortal; no one will find that bad! Don't go to impose a useless constraint on yourself or fear that at each of your motions you are compromising a man of future greatness.

SENNEVILLE: (shyly) Why, milord!

BYRON: Don't be bothered, Mr. De Senneville! I have the right to speak to you thus, because they accuse me of your follies. You are not the only one. As for the rest who ill understand my ideas, add to my misdeeds, those with which you have honored me! But I do not seek a glory that does not belong to me! It would be odd, really, to hear our young folk proclaim satiety as an attribute of genius, boredom as superiority, and as if they got that from me! From me, whose passionate heart was broken against society's pillars! Do you know what this is? I whose thoughts awoke burning under a pale and frozen Sun. Sir, do you know what this indifference is? This pretended disgust with life and its pleasures, this affectation of some of our dandies? It's nullity with its impotence, stupidity with its pretensions, fatuity with its ridicule, and this no more resembles genius then an extinguished lamp resembles the Sun! Ah, leave your soul to its twenty-year-old impressions, if you want to be a man at thirty. See this beautiful sky. Well, let it inspire you. Let these surging masts report your ideas on the shoreless seas, let them spread everywhere, on the affections which have survived them over tempests which have threatened them. Let your thought multiply and impregnate all your impressions rather than extinguish them. That's where life is! That's what poetry is!

(walking toward the Countess and continuing to speak to Senneville while watching her with a caressing air)

Let your heart beat near a woman's! Let yourself feel an unease that no tongue can render, let her hand make yours tremble, let your soul hang suspended over words that escape her lips; let happiness intoxicate you; let sorrow shred you! And perhaps, in these burning emotions, you will surprise some of the mysteries of nature, that it alone reveals to genius, and satiety, not more than affectation will ever have its secret.

(his tone reveals its mockery)

They say, Mr. de Senneville that you were dancing quite marvelously before my stay in Venice. Do, I beg you, as if I were not here.

(indicating the Countess)

This pretty hand is going to belong to you for the first dance. Ah! Don't refuse, Countess, I owe it to him.

(to Senneville) See then! That outfit is charming.

(in a whisper) Child, you were blushing with jealousy. All is not desperate. I am going to cede this little hand to you.

(passing by the Count)

Ours, Count, and from this day!

COUNT: Your burning words will defend our sacred cause,

BYRON: With words! No, no, I must act.

TRELAWNEY: At last our sword is going to demand from the world the place that we are going to occupy in it.

COUNTESS: (smiling) And as for us, we are going to attempt to get there in time to find a ball.

BYRON: Doubtless, Madame. I shall have the honor of seeing you there.

(Exit Countess)

TRELAWNEY: Behold, Milord: the face Guitta is making.

GUITTA Well, I admit it, yes, my heart is not at peace. What can Guitta do before these two great ladies? And yet I don't think I will easily cede to them the love you promised me.

BYRON: Fear nothing. These ladies, you say? The vanity of the one and the coquetry of the other are momentarily amusing, that's all. You, Guitta, you, you pleased me because you loved me without knowing me.

GUITTA: And I love you still, although I know now that you are a hunter like all the damned English! Our Lady, the Holy Virgin, my patroness, will forgive me for it. Now Guitta is no longer mistress of her heart, it is yours.

BYRON: Good Guitta.

TRELAWNEY: The Devil! You are going to soften me up! And yet an affair of an entirely different type must occupy us.

BYRON: He speaks true! Go, my dear child, return to your calm dwelling .Tomorrow, at daybreak, you will see not Byron, but Nolly, your friend.

GUITTA: My friend! That's everything! What's the world, your rank, your fortune to me? Everything is in that word: you love me.

(she stretches her hand)

Till we meet again, Nolly!

BYRON: Till we meet again, Guitta!

(Guitta leaves by the stairway at the back)

BYRON: What naive love! But, say, Trelawney, who's coming now?

WILLIAMS: (entering) A letter for His Excellency.

BYRON: (taking the letter and examining it without opening it) A woman's handwriting! It's unfamiliar to me!

WILLIAMS: (low to Trelawney) Has the gentleman concerned himself with that which I asked of him?

TRELAWNEY: Not yet.

WILLIAMS: Don't forget I beg you. Here's the gentleman.

BYRON: (who has continued to examine the letter) No, I cannot guess who this letter is from, but the handwriting is that of an Englishwoman.

TRELAWNEY: Yet another amorous missive! There's been nothing else for you since your arrival in Venice.

BYRON: (throwing the letter on the divan) That handwriting, those characters. Yes, Trelawney, she's an Englishwoman, but it's not from her! Do you know, do you know that I wrote twenty times, a hundred times for eight years? My friend! And my prayers and my letters all remained without reply. My daughter, my child has been separated from me! She's unaware that I love her! She doesn't know her father!

TRELAWNEY: Still! You seem to have forgotten your humiliations.

BYRON: Listen! I've been able to harden myself to erase her image, because her scorn greeted my love, because she's rejected me, cursed me! Well! Would you believe it, I've never loved anyone but her!

TRELAWNEY: I would never have suspected it.

BYRON: When I read love in Guitta's eyes I cannot prevent myself as I am talking from thinking of another. Ah, if she had loved me thus! Another woman in this country loved me, and I've troubled her life without finding happiness. One single thought is there always! Can you imagine there is a woman who doesn't know how to forgive?

TRELAWNEY: Eh! Eh! Should I tell you all my thoughts?

BYRON: Speak!

TRELAWNEY: Then listen. Your type of constancy to me seems to be the sort women do not appreciate. And Lady Byron must be more delicate than I over your choice of consolation.

BYRON: Lady Byron. Oh, I beg you don't mention that

name, Trelawney! It makes me as ill as a bitter jest. These women, these love affairs, these glories; it's the uproar I've used to choke back her hate which pursues me.

TRELAWNEY: You ought to have succeeded, for the Devil take me, if, at the uproar you have made, you could have heard God's thunder.

BYRON: You are going to annoy me if you make me laugh.

TRELAWNEY: That's better than the other. All the same, milord, our situation has some resemblance. My family imposed an untenable yoke on me. I have planted there my honorable parents with their remonstrances and their kicks! The world is the family of great men, Milord. Its prejudices, its laws, its customs, overwhelm you with their boredom. You abandoned England with its hates, its slanders, its noxious and despotic ideas. All that other men respect and regard as sacred, we are forever debarred from. It's really the Devil, if, after having sent away all boredoms, there remains to us only happiness. What do you think?

BYRON: If the two of us were mistaken, Trelawney?

TRELAWNEY: Bah! Then we would have to become mute, rude in making uproar, the best is that of a cannon..

BYRON: I'll try it. I am so unfortunate!

TRELAWNEY: And what am I?

BYRON: I've often reflected.

TRELAWNEY: As for me, never.

BYRON: Then you have preserved your gayety.

TRELAWNEY: You have consolations.

BYRON: That can escape me.

TRELAWNEY: Others are to be found. This letter, for example.

BYRON: This letter?

TRELAWNEY: Surely it announces to you a new conquest. Take a look! I wager it's some amorous epistle. And love's worth more than marriage for the same reason novels are more amusing than history.

BYRON: Trelawney, do you imagine that I want to play the role of a Lovelace or a Valmont? I don't want that letter! Listen, I wrote once again, to London, to her, to she who bears my name, to her, the mother of my Ada! I am begging her in the name of our child. She will forgive, won't she, Trelawney? She will forgive! And no letter from a woman will be read by me before her reply! Here, take this. See what it is. And if what you suspect is true, I cede her to you.

TRELAWNEY: (going to take the letter) I accept.

BYRON: Open and read.

TRELAWNEY: (reading) "I'm coming from London to see you."

(returning the letter to Byron) Could this be one you have forgotten?

BYRON: (looking at the letter) I don't think so! Continue.

TRELAWNEY: "I'm twenty-six, they tell me I'm beautiful; my heart has never beaten except at your name."

(speaking) Ha, ha! Milord, shall I keep going?

BYRON: Keep going!

TRELAWNEY: (reading) "And the happiness of my life depends on the interview I am asking of you."

BYRON: Now truly, these are our Englishwomen. When they commit a folly, nothing is lacking.

TRELAWNEY: (reading) "But until we've quite understood each other I wish to remain unknown. This letter is written by a different hand, no one knows my name in the hotel I'm dwelling in, across from the Palazzo Oroboni, which you are occupying."

(speaking and pointing to the hotel) Right over there.

(reading) "Tonight, at ten o'clock"

BYRON: It's not far off.

TRELAWNEY: (reading) "During the Countess of d'Oroboni's ball, I will come by the gate which opens on the terrace."

(speaking) This gate here.

(reading) "I will be covered with a veil; don't try to recognize me. I will reveal myself when I am assured that Byron's heart is worthy of me."

BYRON: Worthy of me! In that I recognize English pride which has pursued me with its hate so as not to grant me its praise.

TRELAWNEY: Going once, going twice. The rendezvous remains mine?

BYRON: Yes, for sure! As for me, I am going to prepare myself to go to the ball.

TRELAWNEY: Righto! As for me, I am going to prepare myself to play your part with distinction.

BYRON: I will be really curious to see how you perform it. Try, at least, not to render me ridiculous.

TRELAWNEY: Not too much! Ah, one moment before you leave. I have to speak to you about more serious things.

BYRON: What is it?

TRELAWNEY: Envoys from Greece have requested to see your Lordship; they are hoping in you.

BYRON: And they are right! You know, Trelawney, you know what I've already done to be of use to their holy cause?

TRELAWNEY: No question; a vessel armed at your expense; soldiers raised and paid by you.

BYRON: Greece! Italy! What names! Trelawney, from this moment I feel myself live. My days are no longer consumed in fruitless works for my own happiness, and the happiness of the world. Ah, may heaven second me, and my life will not have been useless.

TRELAWNEY: I was forgetting another mission with which I've been charged.

BYRON: Speak, my friend.

TRELAWNEY: This morning your valet begged me to help him make a large sum of money.

BYRON: How's that?

TRELAWNEY: A certain number of our dear compatriots will give it to him if he is able to place them conveniently to see and hear the illustrious poet Byron.

(Night falls)

BYRON: What folly!

TRELAWNEY: No, by Jove, this is very real! And if your Lordship would lend himself to the circumstances....

BYRON: Now that's admirable! They drove me out, or at least forced me to exile myself from the country, and now they want to pay to see me! You really thought I wouldn't consent to it! Why the idea is bizarre! Come on, night's on us. Goodbye, Trelawney, good luck! You will tell me everything!

(to himself as he leaves) What extravagance! To give money to see me!

(Byron leaves by the door at the right)

TRELAWNEY: (alone) He's laughing! He's more satisfied than he wishes to appear! Ah, there's a man of the greatest character. But the hour of the rendezvous is approaching and he's gone! The Devil! I am embarked on a stupid adventure! I ought to have asked for his advice. I'm sure I'm going to commit some stupidity. I won't know what to say, and he is so used to these things. A rendezvous with a great lady. For there's no doubt she's a great lady. And as for me, who's most beautiful conquest was a little Moroccan princess—

(Night falls completely)

My word she was sweet! We had sacked her country, massacred her whole family and I carried her off on my ship! She loved me to madness! But in this country one cannot be taken in the same manner. It's not the custom. It seems to me I heard a noise from that direction. Ouf! God forgive me, I think I am afraid. Let's move slightly apart. You engage me in a battle where you hide in ambush, and can see the enemy coming. The night is already dark!

(he recoils)

LADY BYRON: (entering through the gate to the terrace) No one! So much the better. My heart is beating so fast that my emotion would have betrayed me!

TRELAWNEY (aside) Come on! She's there!

LADY BYRON: After eight years of separation he no longer recognizes my voice, it's hardly as if the features of my face will have left some memory! And who will suspect me of being in Venice?

TRELAWNEY: (aside) If I could find something nice to begin.

LADY BYRON: Someone's coming, I am trembling.

TRELAWNEY: Don't be afraid, my beautiful lady.

LADY BYRON: Great God!

(she tries to escape, Trelawney stops her)

TRELAWNEY: Oh, don't flee from me, and don't be afraid of anything! By all the devils I am not so terrifying and I expect to justify the good opinion that Byron inspires in you.

LADY BYRON: What are you saying, sir?

TRELAWNEY: Madame, I am saying that you were kind enough to appoint a rendezvous and here I am.

LADY BYRON: You?

TRELAWNEY: Why not?

LADY BYRON: Enough of this, sir! An error that I cannot explain—

TRELAWNEY: (aside) Yikes! Yikes! She wrote that she didn't know him.

LADY BYRON: You are here in place of someone else! In that case allow me to retire without even asking of you an explanation that would be embarrassing and not, perhaps—not very honorable.

TRELAWNEY: I really ask your pardon, Madame. Since the plot is revealed, I will try to justify myself. I admit everything, yes, Madame. Byron, wearied of intrigues and love affairs offered me his place, and that's all.

LADY BYRON: Ah! How mistaken the two of you are as to the purpose of the meeting that I asked of him. But my imprudence shall not be fatal except to me.

TRELAWNEY: Don't desolate yourself, Madame. Trelawney is a brave lad. It shall not be said that he made a woman weep! You see, it's because this scapegrace of a Byron has so many love affairs and successes that as for me, I was quite delighted that he wanted to cede me one! But I am honest, and if at first I was using his name, because that name is a powerful auxiliary, imagine that you would have been quickly undeceived. I would have said to you "You think to love a poet. Not at all, he's a soldier. I've given more blows with sabers than Lord Byron has written verses; does that have the same effect on you?" That's how I would have spoken Madame! Well, what do you think of that?

LADY BYRON: (aside) What language! And are these his friends now?

TRELAWNEY: Listen, Madame. I don't know why you interest me; and I have a wrong to repair towards you. I would even dare to give you some advice! Renounce this damned Lord Byron; he already has three or four love affairs, he—

LADY BYRON: What am I hearing?

TRELAWNEY: He's not much like me; believing in neither God nor the Devil! What do you want? He was unfortunate with his family, with his country! That's what makes us what we are! And what's worse, he had a terrible wife.

LADY BYRON: What do you mean?

TRELAWNEY: All the same, that's neither your affair nor mine, but it seems she was so harsh, so unjust, so mean—

LADY BYRON: His wife?

TRELAWNEY: No question, she! His wife! Ah, I curse her with all my heart for having destroyed all hope and all joy in the most noble of men

LADY BYRON: That's the way his friends belong to him; hate and curses on she who wept so much. Oh, my God!

TRELAWNEY: (watching her closely) Let her not find herself ill now! Madame!

LADY BYRON: (to herself) Got to leave.

TRELAWNEY: She's not listening to me! Madame, it's that, as for me, I know nothing about women who faint.

LADY BYRON: Sir, I have only one thing to say to you.

Tell Lord Byron that it is he, he alone who, listening only to his passions, has offended heaven and raised formidable hate.

TRELAWNEU: Ah, bah!

LADY BYRON: Tell him carefully, that his writings have injured all morality, that divine justice is outraged, and that of men can be implacable.

TRELAWNEY: (aside) It seems she's a devotee.

BYRON: (coming in from the back, stopping, to himself) The meeting is prolonging itself.

LADY BYRON: (to Trelawney) If you are his friend, beg Byron, beg him in the name of heaven, in the name of his wife who pardons him but will never see him again—

BYRON: (aside) What do I hear?

TRELAWNEY: What must I beg of him, Madame?

LADY BYRON: To repent! Goodbye!

(she quickly runs into the hotel)

BYRON: (aside) Who is this woman? And what's she talking about?

TRELAWNEY: (to himself) Ah, really! Does she take me

for a preacher? By Jove, now there's a strange rendezvous! She's gone. Bon voyage! I would have done better to go straight to the Rialto where I was expected.

(he leaves by the stairway to the terrace)

BYRON: (pensively, approaching the hotel) That woman's last words have piqued my curiosity: her voice seemed familiar to me. Ah, now I regret not having attempted the adventure! But this can be fixed. Yes, lovely traveler, who takes so much interest in my well being we will see each other!

(confused sounds in the corridor)

What's that shouting?

VOICES: (off) Lord Byron has been assassinated!

BYRON: Assassinated? Now that's a strange joke. With all the rumors heaped on Byron this is not the least ridiculous.

VOICES: Lord Byron! Lord Byron!

BYRON: Let's go make these clamors cease.

TRELAWNEY: (off) Hey! By all the devils, I tell you I'm not him. Follow me, every one!

(Enter the Countess, the Count, Trelawney, Guitta, and

Mr. de Senneville, followed by a crowd with torches.)

BYRON: (going up to them) What's this uproar signify?

TRELAWNEY: Oh, there you are, Milord.

(to the crowd) Well, you see him! Nothing has happened to the great poet. It was only me who was assassinated.

BYRON: You, Trelawney?

TRELAWNEY: Yes, but they were clumsy. My cloak received everything.

BYRON: And where did they come from?

TRELAWNEY: Ah, you are not lacking in enemies, and there are still jealous husbands in Venice! My devil of an outfit seems so bizarre, but to many represents a great man more than your English frock coat. In the eyes of imbeciles, and they sent me what they destined for you.

BYRON: Dear friend!

TRELAWNEY: I am not even wounded. There were four of them, and without her—

BYRON: Her? Who?

TRELAWNEY: By Jove! Margarita!

BYRON: What?

GUITTA: (who was hanging back, throwing herself in his arms) Byron!

BYRON: What do I see? Wounded?

GUITTA: Nothing! Nothing! I thought they wanted to kill you.

(pulling a dagger from her belt) See, I have wherewith to defend you or follow you.

BYYRON: Good Guitta!

TRELAWNEY: She goes pretty far! An army like that, Milord, and the world is yours!

BYRON: (pressing Guitta to his heart) The world! Do you think it's worth a smile from Guitta? Would it give me even a minute of joy? See, my friend, what glory is!

TRELAWNEY: A power like others, not obtained without peril. But see this crows rushing about at the rumor of your danger.

BYRON: Ah, you are right! Pardon, gentlemen! Ladies, a thousand thanks for your concern!

(to Oroboni) Count, my arm is still yours. I don't know what tells me that I won't die in obscurity in the streets of

Venice.

(whispering) Guitta, go in, bathe your wound, I am offering you asylum in my house.

GUITTA: What happiness!

BYRON: (whispering to Trelawney) Trelawney, I intend to know the name of that woman who was here.

TRELAWNEY: (low) Rely on me.

BYRON: (aloud) Now, let's go to the ball!

COUNTESS: To the ball?

BYRON: Do you want me to embroil myself with the young women of Venice for having interrupted
their joys? No! Let's recommence the dancing and waltzing. According to your system, Madame, pleasures are a compensation for the humiliations of life. Wise men often seek it. Let's not let any be more wise than we.

CURTAIN

ACT II

The stage represents a salon in the Palazzo Oroboni, used as a work room by Byron. Door at the rear opening on a gallery. A table at the left of the audience furnished with writing materials and a candelabra.

AT RISE, Byron is seated at the table; Guitta is seated on a hassock at his feet. Guitta is stringing a necklace, her injured arm is covered with a black bracelet.

GUITTA: (singing) And my love will never leave me.

BYRON: (half laughing, half impatient) Will you get over with that, Guitta? You are preventing me from writing with your blasted refrain.

GUITTA: Hey! There! There! Don't scold.

(she extends her wounded arm to him)

BYRON: (kissing her hand) That wound, it's for me.

GUITTA: Let's not think of it any more, or to put it better

I intend to think of it always! I owe it so much. To be here in your home, to see you at every hour! Because, how you say…?

(singing) No, my love will never leave me any more.

(spoken) I've arranged it on my guitar.

BYRON: Nice! You, too, you make verse.

GUITTA: No! I sing because I'm happy. I say we will never be apart again, because it's my only thought, but as for making verse, I don't even know what it is. I don't know how to read or to write.

BYRON: So much the better for you.

GUITTA: No question! If you know only one thing, you know it better, and to love you is all my science! But Hush! I am distracting you from your grave occupations: come on, Milord, I won't interrupt you any more. Your Excellency can write to his friends.

BYRON: Who told you I am writing to my friends?

GUITTA: In that case, to whom? Surely it's not for folks you've never seen that you are taking the trouble of smearing all over so much paper.

BYRON: (smiling) What would you think, Guitta, if I told you "yes"?

GUITTA: Excellency, I would think that you are amusing yourself to tell me such things, 'cause you think I'm really crazy.

BYRON: Still, if it were true.

GUITTA: Then I would say it's you who are really crazy.

BYRON: Perhaps you would be right! So you don't know what a book is?

GUITTA: Oh, indeed I do! I still have my poor mother's Bible; she was a wise woman, she who read by heart, and when I was small, I heard her reading at night.

BYRON: There are other books beside the Bible.

GUITTA: What use are they?

BYRON: (laughing) What use? My word, not very much, perhaps.

GUITTA: Ah, I get it: they are created to make us happy or better, right?

(triumphantly) And now I understand. You make books.

BYRON: As you say, I make books.

GUITTA: And when people read them, they become good, like you?

BYRON: Poor Guitta! How naive you are!

GUITTA: All the world blesses you?

BYRON: (sighing) You think that?

GUITTA: My mother made us get on our knees to kiss the book of the Evangelist; she said "It's the blessing of the world!"

BYRON: (rising) She did well, Guitta.

(walking about and talking) The young girl's right: what's the point of writing—to write? Nothing. To write, to blame, to criticize, to destroy? Voltaire did everything in that genre. Does there remain something still? Virtue, belief, religion. Those are no more than words.

GUITTA: (standing bolt upright) Holy Virgin! Who is it says that?

BYRON: Hasn't it been repeated around a thousand times, that shout previously heard during the storm by the sailors of Tiberius, the God's have departed. To write, to give men dreams, emotions which surge during this stormy passage in which we live? To cast on the public my sorrow, my un-certitude, the troubles of my soul? Is this the labor which will find a new path for the future of this society that is unfolding? Ah, only those who have left behind them a shining path wherein generations are rushing are truly great!

(disdainfully) But to write today? As for you, Napoleon, you acted. You rebuilt the world.

GUITTA: Hush! Oh, don't utter that name! Do you know he still causes fear here? And you yourself are terrifying me at this moment! I hope I didn't really understand because I thought you were doubting our holy religion! May the Madonna deign to forgive you! I will make a novena so she will protect you, and our love as well.

BYRON: (looking at her for a moment, then passing his hand over his face he sits beside her) Yes, Guitta, let's talk about our love and may the Madonna protect it.

GUITTA: Come, I want to see you write! Will Your Grace deign to read it to me, Milord?

BYRON: You want to hear verse?

GUITTA: No question. And here, this little scroll.

BYRON: (taking it and opening it) Ah, this is not from me. You make me remember: they are verses that the Countess Oroboni asked of me two weeks ago.

(reading) Let's see. Georges de Senneville.

GUITTA: That's that funny little gentleman who's always playing a comedy.

BYRON: Yes.

(reading) "Georges de Senneville to Lord Byron" The impudent, the imbecile. A man who so insults good taste and the conventions cannot write anything worth reading.

(he throws the verse into a box of waste paper.)

GUITTA: (examining) Perhaps he doesn't know what he needs to say to you, Excellency, like me, who for a month called you Nolly! But I hear tell, I recall that men who place importance in titles are very ridiculous. Have you changed your opinion?

BYRON: No, Guitta, no! You don't understand the feeling that animates me.

GUITTA: Oh, indeed I do, I understand perfectly. You speak that way when it's a question of others in general, and it's different when it's a question of you in particular, right?

BYRON: Let's drop that! You want to hear verse, hear this!

(declaiming)

His eyes were shut! He seemed to sigh;
A long shivering made his last breath
This dying Lara, Khaled his young page
Sought life remaining in his noble face.
Then when they raised the mute, pale and icy
From the bloody cadaver with which he was enlaced.

His hand did not snatch the bloody scalp
Whose floating ringlets appeared over his ivory face.
But dry-eyed he shivered and fell motionless
Muttering these words: "He had loved so much!"
Then the sorrowful mystery was revealed
To the faithful page stretched on the ground
They leaned, they hurried, they opened his breast
They wanted to render life to the orphan slave
Whose soul in heaven still rejoices another soul
Vain efforts! He expired, and he was a woman.

GUITTA: A woman in the dress of a page! So as not to leave the one she loved. Ah, that's really fine, I understand that. And when she lost him she died of sorrow! As I would die if you were no more.

BYRON: Good Guitta! And still they said they could not love me, that I was a hard man, cold, whose soul was closed to all good feelings.

GUITTA: Who dared to say that?

BYRON: Someone in whom I had placed all my honor and who destroyed everything! Which left me in bitterness, cruelty, coming from this wound that nothing can cure.

GUITTA: Do you know that this memory alone excites my jealousy?

BYRON: But—I lost her.

GUITTA: Ah! Your heart remains mine, mine alone?

BYRON: Yours, that knows how to love.

GUITTA: Don't be sad. Your sorrow makes me ill. I would give my life to spare you a minute of suffering.

BYRON: Dear and tender friend!

(Enter Trelawney with papers in hand which he tosses on the table)

TRELAWNEY: Damnation! Now there's that man I fought with and killed on account of you who's suing me.

BYRON: (smiling) What! A dead man?

TRELAWNEY: Not by him! The poor devil is quite calm! But his friends, his family, I don't know who. Ah, they'd better watch out! There are some things which make me awfully angry. And I've got a furious desire to take it out on someone.

GUITTA: Have you learned why those assassins wanted his life a week ago?

TRELAWNEY: Yes, by Jove, I've learned it; my word, they were well paid.

BYRON: And by whom?

TRELAWNEY (low) By the husband of the beautiful Marianne. You know?

BYRON: (low) Silence.

GUITTA: What are you saying?

BYRON: That's enough, Guitta, look, I've already enough troubles! Leave me alone with Trelawney for a moment, I beg you.

GUITTA: Come on, I am withdrawing, but I'll be back soon.

BYRON: Yes, soon.

(he shakes her hand, she leaves taking her necklace)

BYRON: What are these papers, my friend?

TRELAWNMEY: Look! This concerns you.

BYRON: (taking the papers on the table) Ah! Newspapers slandering me! Now there's the reward for all my work!

TRELAWNEY: Why can't I rid you of them! What a devilish country where you can no longer even throw your enemy in the crater or burn down his house! I can no longer breathe here. Talk to me about the profession of corsair.

BYRON: Yes, that society stigmatizes with the name

"crime"—the better to conceal its hidden vices or even its hypocritical virtues that no one believes in.

TRELAWNEY: Speak to me of the freedom of deserts or my unbridled horse, wandering the vastness, distracted, wild, without purpose. That's living, that is!

BYRON: And life, such as we've made it in Europe, is so wretched! It's really trouble, truly! When by suppressing childhood, in a type of vegetation, sleeping, eating—time is passed in dressing and undressing.... What remains of real existence? The summer of a monkey, and yet, what's to be done about it? Who the devil was capable if inventing a world like ours, inventing kings, academicians, dandies, and old women?

TRELAWNEY: (smiling) And some young ones who escape us.

BYRON: Ah! You mean the veiled English Lady. That was a week ago. Let's no longer dwell on it! But what do I see? A letter! Trelawney! The address. It's her handwriting.

TRELAWNEY: The handwriting of Lady Byron?

BYRON: You tossed this package in with the others. You didn't suspect, Trelawney? Ah, I don't dare open it! My hand's trembling.

TRELAWNEY: Truly, after the opinion you've given of

yourself, who could think that Lord Byron would be moved to such a degree by receiving a letter—from his wife?

BYRON: My happiness, my future, perhaps, it's in there! Let's see!

(he opens the envelope and finds a sealed letter)

Heavens!

TRELAWNEY: What's wrong?

BYRON: Trelawney—it's my letter! My letter begging her forgiveness in the name of our love in the name of our child! She didn't read it! She didn't open it! Everything is over! But what scorn! What horrible disdain.

TRELAWNEY: Make some calculations, on plans of happiness on the disposition of a woman! That's embarking without a compass to confront the waves and the tempest.

BYRON: No. She will understand me! She will read me despite herself. She didn't want my heart's regrets, my private thoughts addressed to her, to her alone! Well, she will know and everyone will know it, too, with what poignant bitterness she has filled my soul! They will see what a wound she has made, see in this affection broken in my heart—the cause and excuse for my mistakes.

(he sits down to write)

TRELAWNEY: What are you going to do?

BYRON: Leave, leave me alone to exhale into these stanzas the feelings that are overwhelming me, and let the newspaper which will receive them and print them bear them to the eyes of Lady Byron, and despite her, these expressions of my sorrow and my rage!

(writing)

Of all the punishments God has chosen for me is it you that he is arming, Madame Nemesis? But God is not accustomed in punishing crimes to choose an executioner so closely related to his victim.

TRELAWNEY: The Devil! Now there's a promising debut.

BYRON: (writing)

Whoever on earth has known pity
Will be rewarded by pity in heaven.
Not for you who will not let me be heard.
The curse will emerge from my ashes;
For wrongs you have done me—fear to be puffed up by it.
You sow sorrows! You must reap them!

TRELAWNEY: Conjugal gallantry of a new kind.

LORD BYRON:

Pursued by your moralizing spouse Clytemnestra
Rushing to excite envy, to unchain scandal
Because it's you that God charged with punishing me
Sacrificing my present with my future.
Why to speak of a matter, whose cowardly trick
Lies without ever employing a tongue as its accomplice?
Clever subterfuges, silence, hypocritical speech
Nothing is neglected to torture my life.
There you are now, you who created the storm
Standing astride the debris of my sad shipwreck
And your cold heart triumphs, insensitive to my screaming
As a tender heart chokes and dies beneath this wreckage.

TRELAWNEY: If she is not touched by that epistle, after reading it in the newspapers, she'll place it there from ill will.

BYRIN: (rising) That's over with. All the ties are broken. I no longer have a country nor family! My life I can dispose of, my fortune I can employ freely! Let them both serve to free a people enslaved!

TRELAWNEY: Bravo! Danger, battle, we are going to have fun! On this subject I will tell you that Count Oroboni's conspiracy is moving along swiftly; everything is prepared to strike a decisive blow.

BYRON: We will be with him, Trelawney, body and soul.

TRELAWNEY: There's no doubt about that; but will we succeed? Austrian bayonets are numerous, spies are not lacking and Metternich is evil.

BYRON: Well, if yet again a deception awaits us, and if the good cause succumbs, Greece beckons to us, Trelawney! I have not been deaf to her voice. Already, the ship Hercules is in port; it contains arms and part of my fortune. Go! Recruit more soldiers, manage everything. Souls like ours are misunderstood and repressed in this society of petty interests and petty vices barely disguised. We will go to seek a society to be rebuilt on the basis of honor, courage, and virtue. And if I expire, perhaps when cold and frozen my heart reposes under the marble of a tomb, she will repent and take pity on my sorrows.

TRELAWNEY: Give up those ideas! Each time they touch your soul, bitter and desperate thoughts emerge. Think like crazy of glory and happy love affairs. Wait, I didn't tell you that I've had one. I did. To regain the mysterious English lady who escaped us. I don't know what evil genie came to her aid and snatched her from my clutches.

BYRON: I don't want to think about it any more. And besides, only a single element of curiosity is directing me.

(Byron sits, leaning his head in his hands in an abyss of sorrow)

TRELAWNEY: My word, I observed her face. It's pretty.

GUITTA: (entering) Pretty, who's that?

TRELAWNEY: What's it to you? That's my concern.

GUITTA: (uneasy) Are you really sure?

TRELAWNEY: Now there's a suspicion that I am envious of being offended by.

GUITTA: Oh, don't have it in for me! I wish you all the success I don't want him to have.

TRELAWNEY: Your wish doesn't appear to me to materialize. I had reasons. Still, one can have reasons for finding a woman again, especially a pretty woman. I spied her. I learned she's going to leave secretly. I succeeded in winning over the coachman. By my orders he should interrupt her trip by driving her into a ditch.

GUITTA: What are you saying?

TRELAWNEY: Oh, skillfully, without doing her any harm. Only an accident to the carriage in a way so she'll be unable to continue on her way.

GUITTA: The way to Mantua?

TRELAWNEY: Yes. But how do you know that?

GUITTA: Finish.

TRELAWNEY: I must be there, offer my carriage. Ah, yes indeed! She overturns, they call for help. I arrive. The horse, the carriage, the coachman, everybody there, except the lady! Gone, stolen off, impossible to discover her. I don't know what demon—

GUITTA: (laughing) Ah, you didn't know what demon! Well, I have the honor of informing you that it's a familiar demon, very well known to you?

TRELAWNEY: What do you mean?

GUITTA: But you alone are interested in this, right?

BYRON: To prove it to you, Guitta, I don't even want to know who concerns this woman! I leave her to you, and am going to breathe outside for a moment.

(taking a paper with him on which he writes)

GUITTA: How sad he is!

TRELAWNEY: (returning) You were saying, Guitta?

GUITTA: I was saying that the fairy who made the lady vanish is none other than Guitta.

TRELAWNEY: How is that possible?

GUITTA: Oh, my God! It's with the best intentions in the world! I was seated on the bank of the ditch where the coachman honestly earned your money, for the carriage was entirely smashed up and the lady had only a small scratch. But the road is superb. Four feet wide and not the last crowded. The beautiful English lady suspected her escort had good reasons for being so clumsy and her first thought was how to escape him. I ran to her, she came to me and while they were busy righting the carriage we hid ourselves so well behind the neighboring trees that they could not discover us. I escorted her to a secure place, then the next day I brought her back to Venice. She wanted to set out again but an indisposition constrained her to postpone her voyage. For the last week she's lived hidden and unknown to the eyes of the one she accuses of having played her this nasty trick, and I see now it was you. Well, what do you say to that?

TRELAWNEY: I am vanquished. But the lady told you the motives for her stay in Venice? For whom she came? Why was she leaving? You know her rank? Her name?

GUITTA: Me? Not the least in the world.

TRELAWNEY: (aside) I was counting on her to learn everything.

GUITTA: I saw such a lively sorrow depicted on her face to my first questions that I didn't dare to continue.

TRELAWNEY: (aside) He said I wouldn't learn anything.

GUITTA: But from the speech she made when she thought

she was alone, I believe I've guessed at the interest you are displaying today.

TRELAWNEY: What's that?

GUITTA: You ought to know better than anyone.

TRELAWNEY: Me?

GUITTA: And if you tell me everything and I see that I have guessed correctly, well—

TRELAWNEY: Well?

GUITTA: I will help you find her again.

TRELAWNEY: (aside) On that condition I don't risk seeing her very soon.

GUITTA: First of all, you are an infidel, inconstant—

TRELAWNEY: For goodness sakes!

GUITTA: I'm certain of it.

TRELAWNEY: Yeah? Indeed, it's possible.

GUITTA: You abandoned your country, your family, after having given them really great cause for discontent.

TRELAWNEY: I swear to you that they really gave me

some.

GUITTA: You dissipated your fortune.

TRELAWNEY: I had little difficulty in that.

GUITTA: But here's what's most horrible. You left her there, your wife.

TRELAWNEY: Oh, oh! This is very curious.

GUITTA: Don't deny it. Confess, on the contrary. I can fix everything up

TRELAWNEY: You can return my wife to me? And children, perhaps?

GUITTA: Yes, sir! Your daughter, a daughter of seven.

TRELAWNEY: (aside, striking his face) Ah, my god! What a thought!

(aloud) A daughter, a daughter of seven, Guitta? An English girl. Young, beautiful, charming who complains that the one that she loves whose name she bears, who flees is an infidel and she weeps for an ingrate.

GUITTA: That's it, indeed.

TRELAWNEY Ah, Guitta! Return her to her husband, who regrets her, who cannot live without her. It's a joy I implore.

GUITTA: Are you then so soft and suppliant?

TRELAWNEY: But are you really sure that it's she?

GUITTA: First of all she has a sad manner, and so un-happy, it's quite certain she's a married woman.

TRELAWNEY: You think so?

GUITTA: In the midst of her tears she speaks of the con-solation of one who is dearer to her than her life!
Plain to see she's a mother.

TRELAWNEY: And?

GUITTA: And she weeps over an ingrate, ruining himself in this world, and for someone else. It must be you.

TRELAWNEY: Thanks.

GUITTA: She says that she came to Venice to try to touch his heart, to assure herself of the sincerity of his repen-tance, but that she found him so occupied with plans and guilty pleasures that she renounced seeing him ever again and intends to return to London to place an insurmount-able barrier between him and her.

TRELAWNEY: It's she! It's she! But it won't be this way! Guitta, go find her. Depict to her regrets, repentance, spousal remorse that perhaps offended her; let her see him, let her consent to see him.

GUITTA: She won't consent to it.

TRELAWNEY: Tell her that it's a question of his happiness, of his life, of his well-being, whatever you can imagine!

GUITTA: All these fine words will result in no great thing; she will refuse. Still, you've touched me. And she is so sad, so good, that I would like to see her happy. The more one loves the more one forgives! But it's so near! A word, a tear from an ingrate that you were cursing obtains mercy in a minute, an interview is necessary without her suspecting it in advance; she's not far from here. I must bring her without suspecting who she must meet. I am contriving a way. Rely on me.

TRLAWNEY: Wonderful: These women have resources for all difficult circumstances! I agree with your cleverness, Guitta, as well as your good heart, and my gratitude.

GUITTA: Keep that stuff for the salons; I am obliging you! In the like case, you will do it for me, that's all. 'Bye. I'm going to find means to convince her the quickest way possible. Don't get impatient.

(Guitta leaves.)

TRELAWNEY: It's Lady Byron, everything declares it!

She's in Venice! Mysteriously! Who would ever have thought it? In that case she may still love him? But why not answer his letter? Why? Explain who can the heart of a woman! The important thing is that she's here! She has to forgive. Let him find her again since he imagines that his heart is there! Ah, my God! Think of it. A week ago on the terrace, it was she! And he sent me to pay court to his wife. If I had suspected, what then? Come, come, no misfortune took place; everything is for the best! Let him see her again and be reconciled, since he wants to experience marriage again! Is he actually really disgusted with love? On the subject of love, and Guitta! Poor girl! I wasn't thinking of her! She will not be amused by me using her to bring about a reconciliation. Oh, that's a trick to hang for! Word of honor, I hadn't any choice! And if she should take this seriously! Cursed country! Where you cannot do good without doing evil to another, where all interests clash, and cause offense. To the Devil with old Europe! Who will give me Asia! This oriental existence, so sweet and so indolent. The pleasures of the harem after the joys of combat, love without jealousy and uncertainty! Corsair in the seas of India! Happiness is only there! Here, nothing! Hardly the pleasure of smoking a pipe! But I am alone. Let's give ourselves this little relaxation, and await Byron's return. This will put my cares to sleep.

(he takes his pipe)

TRELAWNEY: Some one's coming. Ah—

(continuing to prepare his pipe)

SENNEVILLE (entering) Lord Byron is not here? I am preceding the Countess Oroboni who was hoping to see him.

TRELAWNEY: He's out, sir; and God only knows where he can be found now; he's racing on horseback at the Lido, perhaps, or swimming across the Brenta.

SENNEVILLE: I'm coming to see if he really intended to give some orders, and, if one can, if he permits it, dispose of this salon which communicates with the Palazzo Oroboni at the other end, for the party that's prepared. There's no time to lose.

TRELAWNEY: Yes, yes, dispose away! Parties, comedies, balls, every day! What a life! Suffocating things where you are unable either to breathe or to stroll, and which resemble an unsupportable occupation if one was obliged to perform this occupation in order to make a living. Talk to me about spectacles of Nature! There, throughout, you recognize the power of being supreme and good! But your world, the way you've arranged it, has the appearance of being the handiwork of the Devil gone mad!

(taking a paper from the waste basket and lighting it at the candelabra in order to light his pipe) And I repeat once more: long live the Orient and my pipe.

SENNEVILLE (recognizing his poem) What are you doing?

TRELAWNEY Well, I'm lighting up.

SENNEVILLE: But with what?

TRELAWNEY: With a useless paper.

SENNEVILLE: Pardon! But this poem. Allow me to see it.

TRELAWNEY: (extinguishing the paper and handing it to him) Here.

SENNEVILLE: God! My verses to Byron.

TRELAWNEY: Your verses? If they're no good, they're better employed lighting my pipe than boring the public.

SENNEVILLE: Sir, you will give me satisfaction.

TRELAWNEY: That will be with pleasure, for I truly believe you've lost your reason.

SENNEVILLE: We shall fight, sir.

TRELAWNEY: As much as you like! As for me, that's my profession; I've done nothing else since I came into the world. Shake! You are courageous, that reconciles me to you! Damn! You are a bit ridiculous, a bit affected. You walk as if you were posing for a painting, you speak as if all your words were being taken down by a stenographer, but for the last several years they make such great men from so little that everybody thinks he has the right to become one and places himself on a pedestal in advance! If I have the misfortune tomorrow to put you in the ranks of the gods, that will be your fault.

SENNEVILLE: Curtail these pleasantries, sir. Here's the Countess.

(Enter the Countess)

TRELAWNEY: (extinguishing his pipe) Come closer, Madame. Your compatriot and I don't understand each other. I am leaving you to do the honors of this salon, and I am going to try to find my illustrious friend.

COUNTESS: Then he's gone out?

TRELAWNEY: Yes, and today he's in a fit of ill temper and despair—from which he greatly needs to be distracted.

COUNTESS: Why such little things change the dispositions of his soul! Lord Byron, a bizarre assembly of feelings and the most opposite passions, goes from one moment from the blackest melancholy to the most mad gayety.

TRELAWNEY: I agree the waves of the Adriatic Sea are not more mobile.

COUNTESS: Try to find him. We will attempt to cheer him up.

TRELAWNEY: Would you are able to succeed!

(Trelawney leaves.)

COUNTESS: Have you executed my directions for the party and the arrangement of the palace?

SENNEVILLE: Yes, Madame, and see, already they are lighting up the gallery which Lord Byron has left at your disposal this evening.

COUNTESS: I am really going to force him to amuse himself with us and to agree that the day one has not laughed is the most lost of all. But the gallery is filling with strangers! What's going on?

SENNEVILLE: Lord Byron's valet is with them.

WILLIAMS: (coming forward) Over here! But no noise. They are giving a party and you can place yourselves without being noticed. Ah! Someone's there! It's the Countess.

COUNTESS: What do you want, Williams? Why this company?

WILLIAMS: (embarrassed) These people would like to see Milord's apartment, and I permitted myself.

COUNTESS: Ah, I am there!

(to Senneville) Byron told me this the other day, and he was laughing a lot over it. Perhaps this will be a way of restoring his gayety.

WILLIAMS: I hoped, in the midst of preparations for the party— But if the Countess does not permit—

COUNTESS: Indeed, indeed! I permit! Show them around.

WILLIAMS: How I thank you, Madame.

(goes to the back and brings the strangers in, leading them to one side of the stage. Byron enters from the other.)

BYRON: (stopping) What does this company signify?

WILLIAMS: (to the strangers) It's here, gentlemen, that the illustrious poet composed most of his immortal works, The Corsair, Don Juan, etc, etc.

BYRON: Ah, I understand; it's my scamp of a valet earning his money.

WILLIAMS: It's at this table he sits! And from there emerge his sublime inspirations.

BYRON: Where's all this leading?

WILLIAM: For you know it, gentlemen, and it's not because I have the honor to possess his confidence, but he's the greatest genius who has ever existed.

TRELAWNEY: (entering, seeing Byron) Finally, I've found him.

(Trelawney heads towards Byron who signals him not to budge)

BYRON: Ah, they are paying to see me. Let's amuse ourselves.

ENGLISHMAN: (in the group) You promised us to show him to us himself.

WILLIAMS: Soon, gentleman, I hope.

BYRON: (advancing and low) Silence, scamp!

(taking Trelawney by the hand)

You wanted to see Lord Byron, gentlemen? Here he is!

TRELAWNEY: (recoiling) What?

BYRON: (whispering) Do it, I beg you.

COUNTESS: (to Senneville) What's he saying?

TRELAWNEY: (low to Byron) Pass for you one more time! Thanks, that doesn't work for me.

BYRON: (low) Possibly you'll have more success today.

ENGLISHMAN: (to others) I recognize him from portraits I have seen.

TRELAWNEY: They seem to have been likenesses.

ENGLISHMAN: (approaching Trelawney) Pardon, Milord, if the desire to admire our illustrious compatriot—

TRELAWNEY: Ah, indeed, gentlemen.

BYRON: Oh, you will deny it in vain.

(low) Lend yourself to this mystification)

COUNTESS: (to Senneville) What did I tell you? A joke, and his melancholy vanishes.

BYRON: (to Trelawney) Do you think that a poet might have the face of everyman?

ENGLISHMAN: Oh, no, surely not, and at a glance—

TRELAWNEY: You discovered a true poet in me, right? Celebrity is a fine thing, being known to people who don't know you. And poetry is speaking to people who don't understand you. All that is marvelous.

ENGLISHMAM: (taking Byron aside) You are the friend of Lord Byron?

BYRON: I'm convinced he had no better.

ENGLISHMAN: And all that they say about him is true?

COUNTESS: (to Senneville) I'm afraid that he attracts only bad compliments.

SENNEVILLE: That will be his fault. Let's listen.

ENGLISHMAN: (low) I will admit to you there are vexing rumors about his conduct, his ideas, his principles.

BYRON: Explain yourself.

TRELAWNEY: (aside) I'll bet my pipe he receives a volley of home truths.

ENGLISHMAN: Pardon if I am speaking to you freely, but we would really like to be undeceived! They assure us that he is the enemy of all declared social laws. That he speaks with scorn of all beliefs sacred to mankind, and that he's been on the point of pouring a bitter irony on the wise institutions of our country, old England.

BYRON: (whose face has become a bit animated) Truly? He would have dared? His bold glance would have discovered something that agreed marvelously with the wits of past centuries that could not agree perfectly with men that a succession of events and new ideas had rendered different from their ancestors. And he would permit himself to say what he had seen? Ah, it would be as just to depict the painter as guilty, who, representing the ruins of Venice, for not giving its palaces the splendor and magnificence they once had! Is it Byron's fault he is born in the midst of these centuries of revolution in which societies evolve and rebuild themselves? If his energetic soul's gripped by pity for the puny efforts opposed to the torrent of the ages, which uses and renews everything? And before the great spectacle offered to his gaze, he has had only words of scorn for the platitudes and shabbiness of this society whose hypocrisy excuses vices which do not disturb its appointed order, and represses the noble hearts who dare to free it? Ah, they feel how un-solid is this factitious platform of power, those who want to suffocate the loftiness of souls. It would be more convenient for them, indeed, to impose on men the regular motion, uniform and mechanical of wheels in our mills! But he cannot be compromised by the weight of all their efforts! What would Napoleon have been if space had been lacking for his conquests? There are times and places where the soul cannot find the air it needs for its wings! Where it perishes, where it corrodes because of the food supply! Wherein it seeks and multiplies small interests, small emotions to deafen and forget it is the unworthy goal of life which devours it!

(taking a lofty tone) But in truth, I'm wrong to allow myself to be carried away to speak like this—only ridicule ought to be employed against slander, the only weapon not blighted by the English climate.

ENGLISHMAN: (to the others who look at him dumbfounded) Ah, my God! We've been taken in.

COUNTESS (to Senneville) I was sure he'd betray his incognito.

TRELAWNEY: Lord Byron couldn't have said it better, gentlemen.

RNGLISHMAN: We don't doubt it.

BYRON: You wanted to see and hear this man who is pursued by many petty hates and as many bad passions. Go tell what you have seen to this decrepit society which measures him form below, and to the scribblers who use their teeth to bite at the spurs of his boot, Gentlemen, we are your very humble servants.

ENGLISHMAN: Lord Byron will forgive us for an indiscretion that our admiration ought to excuse.

BYRON: Lord Byron has the honor of saluting you.

ENGLISHMAN: (to Williams low) Who's the other one?

WILLIAMS: (low) I will tell you.

(They all leave with Williams)

COUNTESS: Milord, listening to you I forgot the time for my party, and the cares it imposes on me. I notice my husband who is without question coming to find me.

(Oroboni enters)

COUNT: What's this crowd that's moving away?

BYROM: (smiling) Compatriots who came to gawk at me like a curious animal. I let them—for their money.

COUNTESS: Ah, my dear friend, I was missing you here. You should have heard him.

COUNT: Important duties detained me.

(to Byron) This ball will serve to conceal our plans.

(to Countess) A large number of people have arrived already, Countess; the company is clamoring for you, and the dances are going to begin.

COUNTESS: You are right. But who wouldn't forget around him? Come, I intend for this party to be talked about for a long time in Venice. Come with me, Mr. de Senneville.

(Maskers appear at the back, the Countess goes to greet them)

COUNT: (low to Byron) Hidden under these masks and ball costumes I've brought here all the true children of Italy; they will outwit the caution of our oppressors here in this separated room, they won't find us.

BYRON: I will be here.

COUNT: The weather, the hour, the means of execution, all favor us. Tomorrow, Italy will be free.

BYRON: May it please heaven!

TRELAWNEY: (aside) I won't be able to find a moment to speak to him.

COUNT: See! The numbers are increasing at every moment. Now there is nothing greater or more generous in our imprisoned country. There is the noble Montanari; that one is the singer of Francesca da Rimini.

BYRON: Silvio Pellico.

COUNT: His friend, Maronelli, Menotti, Borell, Villa. May the future realize all that such names promise!

TRELAWNEY: (aside) And Guitta is perhaps going to bring his wife here. Won't he leave?

COUNTESS: (coming towards them) What are you doing there, gentlemen? Come, I beg you, seeing you separated like that they will think you are conspirators, and around here that's dangerous.

COUNT: That's true. Pardon us. Come seek our share of pleasures in the ball. You are coming, Milord?

BYRON: I am following you.

TRELAWNEY: (low) Remain!

BYRON: Come with us.

TRELAWNEY: (low) I have to speak to you.

BYRON: In that case what's wrong? Would you excuse me a word to speak with my friend Trelawney.

COUNT: We are expecting you.

(They leave through the gallery with the Countess. Some Italians are masked, others are not.)

BYRON: Explain yourself quickly.

TRELAWNEY: In this hall, at any moment—

BYRON: Well?

TRELAWNEY: She may come.

BYRON: Who?

TRELAWNEY: She's in Venice. In a few moments, perhaps, you will see her near you, and I hope, forever.

BYRON: Ah, Trelawney, what craziness.

TRELAWNEY: You haven't guessed it. For this trembling hand is hers. Yes, in a moment it will be near it.

Near Lady Byron.

BYRON: In Venice. She? Don't deceive me, I beg you, don't deceive me.

TRELAWNEY: Lady Byron, I tell you is going to come! You can see her, talk to her, she will have to listen to you although she's unaware she's coming to you.

BYRON: Ah, she won't want to listen to me.

TRELAWNEY: Noise in the gallery. Could it be her already?

(going to look)

Yes, Guitta kept her word.

BYRON: Guitta! What's this mean?

TRELAWNEY: I haven't time to explain to you; they're coming.

BYRON: She will flee when she sees me.

TRELAWNEY: Ah, now that's possible. Keep to the side, behind the door. You can see her and hear her.

BYRON: Eight years, Trelawney; eight years of sorrows.

TRELAWNEY: Come, hide, and you will appear after

Guitta leaves. As for me, I'm sneaking off.

(Byron hides behind a door)

They have to listen to each other.

(Trelawney leaves by a different door)

(Enter Guitta and Lady Byron)

GUITTA: Enter, Madame, no one's here.

LADY BYRON: Where are you leading me?

BYRON: That voice. A week ago I didn't recognize it.

GUITTA: Fear nothing, Madame.

(aside) Now where is he? No question he wanted me to prepare the interview.

LADY BYRON: You say you'd like to keep me at a distance from news that would trouble my peace, give me a peaceful retreat for the two hours that remain for me to spend in this unfortunate city of Venice, where I ought never to have come. I followed you because you promised me that from the new apartment chosen by you, I could leave without being seen by anyone thus escaping my persecutors. This illuminated salon, the uproar which reaches me, startles me. But Guitta, you yourself seem uneasy; you are seeking, you are expecting someone. Oh, would you have betrayed me? What do you want from me? Where am I? Why did you bring me here?

GUITTA: I implore you to forgive me.

LADY BYRON: Forgive you! What for?

GUITTA: I deceived you.

LADY BYRON: You are terrifying me.

GUITTA: It's for your happiness.

LADY BYRON: What do you mean?

GUITTA: He loves you, misses you, wants to see you.

LADY BYRON: What are you saying?

GUITTA: I know all about it! Haven't I seen your sadness when I sought to distract you from your sufferings? Ah, my heart was not deceived by it! The greatest of your sorrows came from the soul! You were so sweet and kind to me! Judge my happiness when I learned that someone missed you, and loved you still in secret, as much, at least, as he was loved.

BYRON: (hidden) What do I hear? And it's Guitta—

GUITTA: That all his desires were to see you again.

LADY BYRON: Never.

GUITTA: To implore a pardon that you cannot refuse.

LADY BYRON: Who gave you the right to speak to me like this?

GUITTA: Your misfortune! You are in pain! Another is suffering more than you! To bring two hearts together made unhappy by absence, that's what poor Guitta wants to attempt. I am only an obscure girl, I know it, but me, too, I'm in love, and if the one my heart has chosen was separated from me, I would bless the hand that reunited us.

BYRON: What a strange mystery. Of whom is she speaking?

LADY BYRON: Listen to me, Guitta. I owe you a lot, you saved me from a peril and your affectionate attentions have touched my heart. I have imposed the rule of shutting in forever the funereal secret of my sufferings. I am unaware how I revealed them, but you alone in the world know that I secretly left the retreat where I wept alone, for eight years! The letters from the man who offended me so cruelly spoke of repentance. I resisted for a long while, Finally, I gave in. I left. What did I see on my trip to Venice? Ah, know, too, that convinced of his misdeeds I distanced myself without seeing him again and without forgiving him.

GUITTA: Oh, no, Madame! That solitary life you have

led, this trip you took, that troubled voice when speaking of him, all tell me that you love him, still. Oh, you will forgive! He must come, where can he be? Why doesn't he reveal himself? I've got to find him and I will bring him.

(She leaves, and Byron appears)

LADY BYRON: (seeing him) It's him!

BYRON: (to Lady Byron) You here? You!

LADY BYRON: (joyfully) Byron!

BYRON: But these cruel reproaches, these offensive words about unforgivable wrongs—

LADY BYRON: Can I remember them myself in his presence?

BYRON: You'll forgive?

LADY BYRON: I'll forget.

BYRON: And you love the one that you've repulsed for so long?

LADY BYRON: His country is calling him back! Will he renounce all other interests, all other hopes? Follow her to London?

BYRON: I swear it.

LADY BYRON: (extending her hand to him) I'm yours, Byron! And forever!

GUITTA: (returning and coming between them) What do I hear? Him! You!

LADY BYRON: What's the matter with you, Guitta?

BYRON: All is discovered.

GUITTA: But it isn't. It cannot be.

BYRON: (distressed) Guitta.

GUITTA: (wildly distracted) Has my reason abandoned me? I don't understand a thing.

(to Byron) Why are you here? What are you doing here?

(to Lady Byron) The man that you loved, that you were seeking, who is the father of your child—where is he?

LADY BYRON: That's him! Didn't you know it?

GUITTA: What! The wife he still adored despite her cruelty and disdain?

LADY BYRON: That's me!

GUITTA: (uttering a scream) Oh, but that's not true! It's not possible.

(drawing her dagger from her belt) Say that it's not true!

BYRON: (snatching her dagger from her) Guitta! Wretch! What are you going to do?

GUITTA: Ah! I see it all now! I've been unworthily deceived. Oh, this is infamous!

BYRON: Guitta.

GUITTA: I repeat to you: this is infamous! But don't be afraid. She is the mother of your child. My God! He loves her. Come, I'm one too many here.

LADY BYRON: What distraction!

GUITTA: Milord, poor Guitta forgives you. Goodbye!

(Guitta leaves in disorder)

BYRON: (taking a few steps to follow her) Oh, I won't stand for it.

LADY BYRON: (in a tone of reproach) Ah! Milord.

BYRON: (aside) What to do?

(Enter Oroboni and the Italian conspirators)

COUNT: Byron, we are rushing to you; you must act.

BYRON: Now! No, no!

(going to Lady Byron)

No more battles! No more glorious plans.

COUNT: What do I hear? If we delay, everything is lost. Your aid, your advices, your arm, instantly.

BYRON: Ah! What I've wanted so much. But Great God, at what a moment.

LADY BYRON: (with terror) Byron, what's going on now?

BYRON: May heaven be damned for thus fulfilling my wishes. But it won't conquer me.

(to Count) The signal's been given?

COUNT: (pointing to a conspirator) Mescantini must sound the tocsin from the Church of Saint Mark.

BYRON: Let him be on his way! And you, gentlemen, disperse. Each to his post! Me, especially. The place of re-grouping, the ship *Hercules* wading in port. The password to get aboard, my motto: "Ride Byron!" The rally word for fighting: "Liberty."

ALL: (in a hushed voice) Liberty! Liberty!

(Trelawney entering)

TRELAWNEY: Liberty? Do you know what liberty is in this country and what that word produces? Ten thousand foreign bayonets encircle the palace where you dared to pronounce them.

ALL: Heavens!

BYRON: (with bitter irony) Fine! It had to be this way, gentlemen! Your cause was that of honor: you had only courage and virtue going for you. In that case how could you succeed?

LADY BYRON: (aside) Still meddling in conspiracies.

COUNTESS: (entering with the crowd of guests from the ball) Count, doubtless you know soldiers are surrounding the palace and I have guessed—

COUNT: I've done my duty.

COUNTESS: And I know mine.

SENNEVILLE (rushing in) Margarita Cogni just hurled herself from the height of the terrace into the canal.

BYRON: (rushing toward the terrace) Just heaven!

TRELAWNEY: (to Senneville) And you didn't leap in after her?

SENNEVILLE: I don't swim.

BYRON: Help me, Trelawney. She must be saved at all cost.

(as they are about to leave, all exits are blocked by Austrian soldiers; a drum roll outside)

AUSTRIAN OFFICER Absolutely no one whatsoever can leave.

TRELAWNEY: We'll see about that! (kicking one soldier in the leg, and pushing another aside, and shoving a third. He escapes shouting) Don't worry, Milord. I am going to save Guitta.

AUSTRIAN OFFICER: I've received an order to arrest Count Oroboni, and all the Italians present, too. Lord Byron because of his English character will be free tomorrow.

LORD BYRON: I thank the cannons of the English Fleet. It is a shame that Justice, to make itself understood, has not a voice as powerful as theirs.

(General consternation; the curtain falls)

CURTAIN

ACT III

Same set as Act II.

Trelawney is standing. The Countess is seated near Guitta who is on the divan.

GUITTA: (sad and pensive) She was his wife!

COUNTESS: Don't think about it any more, Guitta! Heaven, that you pray to each morning with so much fervor will come to your aid; it will erase his cruel memory.

GUITTA: Yes, I want to forget him. But, Trelawney, why save me?

TRELAWNEY: Now that's a nice question! A whole army would not have succeeded in preventing me.

GUITTA: What has happened here since yesterday?

COUNTESS Austrian troops surrounded the palace in the midst of the ball; the rest of the night was spent questioning in the shadows and the mystery of all those who were here; some are already released but Count Oroboni and his most intimate friends are still locked in a room in the palace where no one is allowed in. I still hope that there's no proof against them and soon they will be returned to their families.

TRELAWNEY: May it please God!

COUNTESS: Ah, he'll have to flee Italy. We will leave, we will go to France, once the Count is free. I will bring you, Guitta, that's agreed with him. Isn't it true that you will come?

GUITTA: (dreary and distraught, then taking the hand of the Countess excitedly) Oh, it's impossible that that frigid Englishwoman loved him like me. He misses me, right?

TRELAWNEY: I am expecting him. We have a rendez-vous. Hey, hold on, here he is.

COUNTESS: Come closer, sir. They say you are preparing to leave.

SENNEVILLE: After I've chalked a few moments with this gentleman, if I still have, after that, a few conversations to make, it will be outside this country.

COUNTESS: (pulling him aside) If I were to demand a great service of you?

SENNEVILLE: Madame, you know that a word from you

would prevent my departure.

COUNTESS: If I begged you to protect our flight?

SENNEVILLE: You! You would return to France? Oh, Madame, my life is at your disposal. If this gentleman has not disposed of it in a moment.

COUNTESS: What's that signify?

TRELAWNEY: Nothing, Madame! A childish quarrel! But it can be straightened out.

(to Senneville) Young man, this is no doubt your first affair, and you intend to show your courage. That's quite fine. As for me I don' have the same motives, and besides, other grave concerns demand my time. Therefore, listen. Today's the twenty-fifth of March 1823. The twenty-fifth of March 1825 I will be in Paris, and we will see each other again, and if your anger still lasts, we can resume the conversation where we left it today. Shake?

SENNEVILLE: So be it, sir.

(aside) A voyage with her.... What happiness!

COUNTESS: Come, Guitta; Mr. de Senneville, give me your hand. I am going to explain what I expect from your kindness; we must leave this country as soon as possible. (she goes in through the door at the right)

TRELAWNEY: Yes, I too must leave this country. But alone! When I hoped to leave with Byron! At last, he is happy! He believes it. I have nothing to regret! It's he I perceive. How dreamy he is. He doesn't even see me. Let's not interrupt him: wait!

(Trelawney remains apart.)

BYRON: (entering without seeing Trelawney) I am happy! Yes, certainly! Here I am arrived at the fulfillment of my dreams. I am happy. My soul had coursed through all parts of life in search of happiness, and no part was encountered on my path. Perhaps it is actually only in these long frequented ways where up to now I have disdained to march? Perhaps, the lengthy experience acquired before is worth more to us than this burning impatience whose agitation has wearied my life? Yes, now at last, rest! These plans formed for the deliverance of Italy must be renounced. All is finished on this side! Poor Guitta! Ah, drive that idea away! Her decision to leave with the Countess, her resignation return to me the calm I sigh after. My wife, my companion, the one who bears my name is here, Soon I am going to see my Ada again, my child!

TRELAWNEY: (coming forward) Truly, I don't know if the old friend of a bad actor may still dare to greet you, even with the deepest respect, such a respectable family man.

BYRON: Ah, there you are, my joyous companion.

TRELAWNEY: Joyous, yes! But your companion, no! You are entering into paths of wisdom, the Devil if I know how to follow you down that path.

BYRON: Don't I have to give up the profession of young man, at last, and cede my place to others?

TRELAWNEY: Where have you seen, if you please, anyone cede a good situation without being asked to do so? As for me, I imitate our statesmen. I am keeping mine as long as possible. And so as to busy my fine days, I am going to risk them for the deliverance of Greece.

BYRON: Since 1814, I've often thought that the world is worthy neither the trouble it takes to conquer it, nor regrets experienced in quitting it.

TRELAWNEY: (with irony) Oh, surely! Better to live as an honest bourgeois, breathe at one's ease in a large armchair of his grandfather, busy with repairing his old castle! To divert oneself, one still has the county assemblies, then from time to time although rarely, from fear of contracting gout through dissipation, one can give oneself the pleasure of hunting a fox and all year, for goodness sake, hate your neighbors and scorn the human race.

BYRON: (half smiling) Would you shut up, Trelawney! I tell you that I am happy! Wearied of this wandering life, without rest, without consideration, which has filled my soul with bitterness, weary of these love affairs which bring with them only trouble and regret I want to find happiness in bonds forged by respect, in calm, in peace.

TRELAWNEY: That I wish you, along with paradise at the end of your life. As for me, not being so wise, I am going to attempt to amuse myself once again, and if your Grace wants to leave at my disposition the boat which was to take us to Greece, I will attempt it alone—

BYRON: Don't speak to me of that, Trelawney! Mercy! Ah, I ought to run towards that noble country whose people are shaking their fetters in the hope of breaking them. The duty of helping to break an odious yoke. There I would have given asylum to liberty that they would banish from the world! To this much called after Liberty, so coveted by nations, I would offer either my death or my glory. That was a noble plan! But, no, no! That glory would have been like others, illusory, deceitful, and cruel. What matter that one more name survive in centuries to come? I've renounced it! Go, my friend, depart, dispose of everything! But Mercy, don't speak to me of it any more! I have told you: my goodbyes to renown, genius, glory are without return! Execute, by yourself, the plans we'd formed together; lead those soldiers who are waiting for me; don't let them know all the plans that occupy me! To govern men, you mustn't precede their ideas but follow them. So, Goodbye! Don't remain here any longer. Your presence reminds me of everything I wish to forget. I am not speaking to you of myself! You know often repeated, one is often happy or unhappy in this world because of things one doesn't or cannot, speak of. But at this time, at least, if happiness is not to be forced, it won't be for the fault of having remained idle while waiting for it.

TRELAWNEY: Now there's great wisdom that I fear may prove a folly. But I'm shutting up. These things are not within my purview. And now then, goodbye. Let me shake your hand again, Byron! One day the world will know completely the genius of a great poet, I alone, perhaps, will have known the soul of the best of men.

(turning his head and wiping away a tear)

BYRON: (shaking his hand) Trelawney, my friend.

TRELAWNEY: He's the best! It makes me ill. Come, I will leave this very day. I need some cannon fire to ease all this! Goodbye!

(Exit Trelawney)

BYRON: (alone) He was a friend! And how many can one find in life? Yet another sacrifice to Lady Byron. To her, to her repose, to her happiness! I promised everything. Her love will suffice in place of everything. Who's coming? Ah, it's Guitta.

GUITTA: (pale and languishing) Oh,—don't move away, Milord. It's no longer this woman who is in despair; it's a poor girl who's coming to a last sad goodbye, trembling, to the one who loved her.

BYRON: Guitta, you see how it afflicts me.

GUITTA: Don't fear my reproaches! No, it's all over for the unfortunate Guitta. She had beautiful days! They were short, it's true, but they composed her whole life! Those that preceded them don't count for her. Those that follow will be engaged in remembering them, reliving in her mind all the moments wherein she saw you, all the words that she heard you say. You remember when you said: "Guitta, I love you"? Well, I still hear those words! It's the same voice, the same inflection! I will have them with me as if you said them to another. They will remain there. I know well enough it's all an illusion. But they will last longer than my happiness.

BYRON: (to himself) I was prepared for her reproaches, but I cannot endure this deep, calm sorrow.

GUITTA: Why turn your eyes away? Are you afraid to look at me? Oh, at least don't hate me!

BYRON: Hate you, my poor child!

GUITTA: No, that voice is sweet, it is like that I expected to hear it saying endlessly: I love you. Oh, Nolly, Nolly, if you could say it one more time, it seems to me, I would die content.

BYRON: Ah! Why does heaven send me such tests? Guitta, Guitta, we must part! For I will lie, I will be false and deceitful, if I refuse to tell you: I love you. Go away! Go away instantly!

GUITTA: Ah! I don't envy anybody anything now! Don't hide from me that expression of tenderness and sweetness that, despite you, I see in your face! O my God! This poor girl has the power to confer happiness or sorrow on this man who's so much superior to her. Superior to all! For they admire you, they envy you! And as for me, I love you. But that's not enough to pay for a sorrow in your heart! What more can I do?

BYRON: Guitta, you loved me with a true, tender, sincere love. Go my child. That's a lot, that's everything.

GUITTA: Listen, for a joy like that of being loved by you, there must be a devotion that nothing can equal.

BYRON: What do you mean?

GUITTA: I loved you and what woman would not have done as much? But you know me, you know how proud and jealous Guitta was! Well, that jealousy which seared my heart, I kept it shut in, those words of love which escaped my lips when I saw you, I will hold them back! My eyes will turn away from yours, my hand will no longer seek your hand, I will stay here near you, frigid, unfeeling, like the marble of our statues, but I will be there. You will allow me to remain.

BYRON: You, Guitta?

GUITTA: Oh, don't be frightened. Guitta will only be that poor girl who takes care of Lady Byron.

BYRON: What! You would—?

GUITTA If you leave without me, I will be forever unaware if you are happy! Oh, let me follow you, but like a slave! Hidden in a corner of your house, I will see you.— sometimes, from a distance. I will know you, and these oceans won't separate us. I will be able to hear your voice.

BYRON: Ah! Don't think of that. What you want is impossible.

GUITTA: But I will love her. I will serve her. I will see her loving you and I will say nothing! Then she won't believe in my love. The whole world will forget it. Except me! I will be calm! No glance, however attentive it may be will be able to guess what's happening there! I will see you near her speaking to her of love. And my eyes will remain dry. You can press her to your heart in front of me and she won't see me go pale. Now do you believe I love you?

BYRON: I never doubted it!

GUITTA: Go, it's something to be loved this way! Over whom would you have the same rights, the same empire? Who would give you more than her life?

BYRON: In the name of Heaven! Stop! I don't want to hear it, I cannot! It's I, I who beg you, Guitta. Don't talk this way any more!

GUITTA: (joyfully) I was wounding you then?

BYRON: (striding, to himself) Ah, the past leaves indelible traces. Will I find in my past mistakes invincible obstacles to my future plans?

GUITTA: What's he saying?

BYRON: No, no! My soul is unworthy of its own wound. All these bonds that enchain me, I will have the courage to break. Listen, Guitta.

GUITTA: God! Now how frigid and severe you are.

BYRON: (bitterly) That love you are expressing, that very vivacious exaltation, like other illusions will one day perish from disgust and boredom! Isn't it better to break the shining leaf than see it fall and wither? Leave, Guitta, leave. It's a last goodbye.

GUITTA: What a change in the expression of your features. What's happened?

BYRON: Poor child!

GUITTA: (going to sit on the divan, weeping) My heart can no longer understand a thing.

COUNTESS: (entering) What do I see? Guitta here! Next to you.

BYRON: For the last time.

COUNTESS: Milord, I am coming to solicit your complaisance.

BYRON: Speak, Madame.

COUNTESS: The authorities are preparing to leave: they are making sure that no evidence allows them to curtail Oroboni's freedom any longer, or that of his friends, and I've conceived a plan that you can render feasible in the midst of surveillance which will dog Oroboni's steps.

BYRON: How's that? Would you explain?

COUNTESS: I want to snatch my husband from perils by taking him to France. Mr. de Senneville will grant me the passport requested for himself, and while the crows that seek you fill this palace we will be able to escape, I hope from the suspicions of vigilance that surrounds us. A similar opportunity may never be found again! Do you consent to it?

BYRON: Ah, I will never forgive you if you hesitate for a minute to believe so. Come on, let this poetic talent at least serve the well being of a proscribed man! Dispose of me and my actions, and may happy days shine on you in the land of France!

COUNTESS Come on, Guitta, We will see each other again, Milord.

GUITTA: Let's go, Madame, come. One moment more and I may not have the strength to leave. Goodbye, Milord.

(the women leave)

BYRON: Ah! My face never paled! My heart never knew fear, and now I'm trembling. It seems that my destiny is going to be accomplished! There's something decisive and immovable about this day! Still, all that was cruel. Isn't it over? Are not the sacrifices made? Don't I see coming to me forever, she who is the reward for all these sacrifices, she that I've missed for eight years, she who is going to give me at last peaceful, pure and happy days?

(Enter Lady Byron)

BYRON: (affectionate, tender) Ah! You are here! It seems to me that I've returned to that day when Miss. Milbank deigned to listen to the vows of Byron.

LADY BYRON: (cold, constrained, holding a newspaper in her hand) Ten years have passed since then, Milord, and yet it is also present in her memory! If few beautiful days have shone for her it has not eradicated the day she dared to call happy—or unhappy.

BYRON: Ah—Say happy.

LADY BYRON: Alas!

BYRON: Today in which the hand of my cherished companion trembles in mine.

(taking her hand) Ah, I see with joy this ring has never left your hand! This ring, you recollect it? It was my mother's! For several years it was lost, and miraculously found the eve of our marriage. In it I thought I saw a presage of happiness.

LADY BYRON: Your mother's marriage wasn't happy! And this ring was destined to become the seal of an alliance yet more unhappy.

BYRON: Don't say that! Abandon your coldness and severity. Yesterday your glance was softer. Look at me like yesterday.

LADY BYRON: Yesterday I believed your words.

BYRON: Why would you doubt them today?

LADY BYRON: Because they are false and deceitful.

BYRON: You don't believe that!

LADY BYRON: I have proof of it.

BYRON: You?

LADY BYRON: Me.

BYRON: That's impossible.

LADY BYRON: (presenting a newspaper to him) Wait, here—look.

BYRON: God.

LADY BYRON: Must I read them to you myself, these verses that are going to instruct all Europe about your true feelings toward me?

BYRON: (to himself) Misery! And I had forgotten! Ah! All is over.

LADY BYRON: These imprecations of your hate have been read everywhere already, while you were assuring me of your love.

BYRON: Heaven has punished me and by means of my own words.

LADY BYRON: I will not reply to these odious slanders! But you now see what could be for me deceitful words that sought to convince me—who came to read in the depth of your thought!

BYRON: Ah! That's not the depth of my heart! Even the violence of these reproaches attests to the despair which distracts me.

LADY BYRON: (very cold) Nothing more, Milord! If my

heart has found its most pitiless enemy in its most intimate and cherished affections, then it must be allowed to close itself up forever.

BYRON: Then it's true! The past has forever destroyed the hopes of the future! Returning to what I have lost has become impossible?

LADY BYRON: Still, Milord, I promised yesterday, I will keep all my promises! My forgetting the past will force on the world a seeming forgetfulness, You will resume the rank which is your due. You will find your daughter again, she only knows how to weep for you. And you won't hear any reproach from the one that a cruel destiny named your wife.

BYRON: (bitterly) Ah! No doubt! I will see her submissive and resigned, right?

LADY BYRON: Submissive and resigned.

BYRON: Without any memory of love. Is it not true?

LADY BYRON: With no memory of hate, nor love.

BYRON: Not counting on happiness?

LADY BYRON: No longer hoping for it except in heaven.

BYRON: Not loving anything on earth.

LADY BYRON: There still remains my child.

BYRON: (overwhelmed) Ah!

LADY BYRON: (aside) My heart is broken. Let's get out of here.

(aloud) Milord! I shall await your orders.

(she leaves with some emotion)

BYRON: Fine! Now there's the last punishment heaven was reserving for me! My God, you know if that despairing resignation would not be an eternal torture for me! Ah, it's time for this heart to freeze since it has ceased to move the heart it wanted to touch! Terrible and irreconcilable destiny—do you admit no pardon? I will perish struggling against your decrees!

(his face becomes animated and seems to make a sudden decision)

But I will not perish completely. Something of me will remain! And until my death, nothing will have been profitless and fruitless! Forward. Behind me the road is blocked. Forward, then. Now everything is decided.

(writing in his notebooks)

Williams!

(Williams enters)

These notebooks to Trelawney and don't lose a moment.

(Williams leaves)

My future is fixed.

COUNTESS: (Countess enters, and behind her the crowd which increases little by little in the background) Milord, I've put your kindness to profit.

BYRON: You did well!

(low) And everything is prepared?

COUNTESS: (low) Everything. I expect no more than my husband's freedom: in the midst of this crowd we will pass unnoticed.

BYRON: (low) Count on me!

(to crowd) Hospitable Venetians who have softened the bitterness of my pains, come receive the goodbyes of Byron. But it is not for his cold and ungrateful country that he's going to quit these delightful climes.

COUNTESS: What do you mean?

BYRON: Fatality is in it! It's to old Europe that I address today this solemn goodbye! All come close and here these verses. The last that this beautiful heaven has inspired in me.

(declaiming)

I was born on soil where a man is proud to be born.
Hate proscribed me. I left. Perhaps one day.
They will come to seek the imprint of my step.
Land of my ancestors, I do not curse you.
But may my heart freeze before I forget you,
Country, loved by heaven, noble beautiful Italy!
Where I've poured out tears over your captivity
Old cradle of glory and liberty.
Ah, grand memories, mother august and fruitful
Your fatal history is the history of the world!
Italy arises, it reigns! Its voice
Awakes an infant nature and makes it thunder to its rights,
Soon its scepter falls into the hands of victory
The shaken universe shivers. And when Glory
Has squandered the blood and gold of nations,
Vices, cares and corruption
In their turn devour the heritage of glory;
Then behind them slavery stands and grows larger.
Ah—you will shake off the chains that affront you.
Queen of beauty, Queen of harmony
In your fields, heroes will be consoled, reborn
And your crown rejuvenated
With an immortal dazzle that will shine on your face!
And you, Venice, Goodbye! On this peaceful sea
Standing straight like a vessel on a motionless anchor
You appeared to me! Alas joyful songs—

The mute Rialto no longer hears these sweet sounds!
Once your head has passed thirteen centuries of glory
What remains of it? Hardly a page of history.
But the raucous accents of Northern slaves
Will awaken one day, your old sleeping lion!
And then, demanding blood instead of tears
His lengthy roars will call you to arms.
For other oppressed dead in other climes.
At the bottom of my skull I will not hear it
Then Venice, remember my last goodbye.
One mustn't weep over this chain, one must break it!

(the crowd applauds Byron)

COUNTESS What noble accents. In that case, why meddle with omens so funereal? We will see each other again in happier times.

BYRON: Something tells me I will not return from the land of Homer and Themistocles.

SENNEVILLE: (entering, in a low voice to the Countess) Everything's prepared for your departure.

COUNTESS: (low) Wait for my husband! I know the interrogation has been terminated; he's going to be returned to me. And hold on. Soldiers are leaving the palace.

BYRON: (to Trelawney) There you are, my friend. What do I see? Guitta?

TRELAWNEY: Yes, Milord, when your notebooks were delivered to me, in my joy, I was unable to hide from her that you were coming to Greece to battle with us!

GUITTA: And Guitta remembered the page in Lara. Here she is, Byron, by your side, always and forever.

BYRON: Darling, Guitta.

TRERLAWNEY: The Hercules is only awaiting the presence of Lord Byron to set sail.

COUNTESS: But what do I see?

BYRON: O heaven!

(Austrian soldiers arrive, pushing the crowd back and to the sides)

COUNTESS: (going to her husband) They said you were going to be free. The wretches deceived me.

COUNT: They feared your actions and your prayers.

COUNTESS: They said there were no proofs.

COUNT: Doesn't it suffice to haves a suspicion?

COUNTESS: Wretch!

COUNT: Glory! Liberty! Country! Nothing remains to

me!

COUNTESS: A wife who loves you, Oroboni, who will follow you, and soften your noble captivity.

BYRON: And the future will avenge you.

COUNT: Goodbye, Byron. I am going to find death in Spielberg prison.

BYRON: Goodbye, Oroboni! I am going to seek death for the freedom of Greece!

CURTAIN

ABOUT FRANK J. MORLOCK

FRANK J. MORLOCK has written and translated many plays since retiring from the legal profession in 1992. His translations have also appeared on Project Gutenberg, the Alexandre Dumas Père web page, Literature in the Age of Napoléon, Infinite Artistries.com, and Munsey's (formerly Blackmask). In 2006 he received an award from the North American Jules Verne Society for his translations of Verne's plays. He lives and works in México.

www.ingramcontent.com/pod-product-compliance
Lightning Source LLC
LaVergne TN
LVHW011208080426
835508LV00007B/676